ENCYCLOPEDIA OF GOOD HEALTH

SUBSTANCE ABUSE

ENCYCLOPEDIA OF GOOD HEALTH

SUBSTANCE ABUSE

Series Editors

MARIO ORLANDI, Ph.D., M.P.H.

and

DONALD PRUE, Ph.D.

Text by

ANNETTE SPENCE

Facts On File Publications

New York • Oxford

A FRIEDMAN GROUP BOOK

First published in 1989 by Facts On File Publications, Inc.
460 Park Avenue South
New York, New York 10016

Library of Congress Cataloging-in-Publication Data

Spence, Annette.
Substance abuse.

(Encyclopedia of good health)
Includes index.
Summary: Discusses the effects of tobacco, alcohol, and drugs, and social aspects such as peer pressure to abuse these substances.
1. Youth—United States—Substance use—Juvenile literature. 2. Substance abuse—United States—Juvenile literature. [1. Smoking. 2. Alcohol. 3. Drug abuse] I. Title. II. Series: Spence, Annette. Encyclopedia of good health.
HV4999.Y68S64 1988 362.2′9 87-21142
ISBN 0-8160-1669-0

British CIP data available upon request

ENCYCLOPEDIA OF GOOD HEALTH: SUBSTANCE ABUSE
was prepared and produced by
Michael Friedman Publishing Group, Inc.
15 West 26th Street
New York, New York 10010

Designer: Rod Gonzalez
Art Director: Mary Moriarty
Illustrations: Kenneth Spengler

Typeset by BPE Graphics, Inc.
Color separated, printed, and bound in Hong Kong by South Seas International Press Company Ltd.

1 3 5 7 9 10 8 6 4 2

About the Series Editors

Mario Orlandi is chief of the Division of Health Promotion Research of the American Health Foundation. He has a Ph.D. in psychology with further study in health promotion. He has written and edited numerous books and articles, among them The American Health Foundation Guide to Lifespan Health *(Dodd Mead, 1984), and has received numerous grants, awards, and commendations. Orlandi lives in New York City.*

Dr. Donald M. Prue is a management consultant specializing in productivity improvement and wellness programs in business and industrial settings. He was formerly a senior scientist at the American Health Foundation and holds a doctorate in clinical psychology. He has published over forty articles and books on health promotion and was recognized in the Congressional Record *for his work. Prue lives in Houston, Texas.*

About the Author

Annette Spence received a degree in journalism from the University of Tennessee at Knoxville. Her articles have appeared in Redbook, Weight Watchers Magazine, Cosmopolitan, *and* Bride's, *and she has contributed to a number of books. Spence is associate editor for Whittle Communications, a health media company in New York City. She lives in Stamford, Connecticut.*

C O N T

How to Use This Book • page 8

P A R T I

What's Important For Me To Know About Substance Abuse? • page 10

E N T S

PART II

How Can I Avoid Or, If I Have To, Handle Substance Abuse · page 96

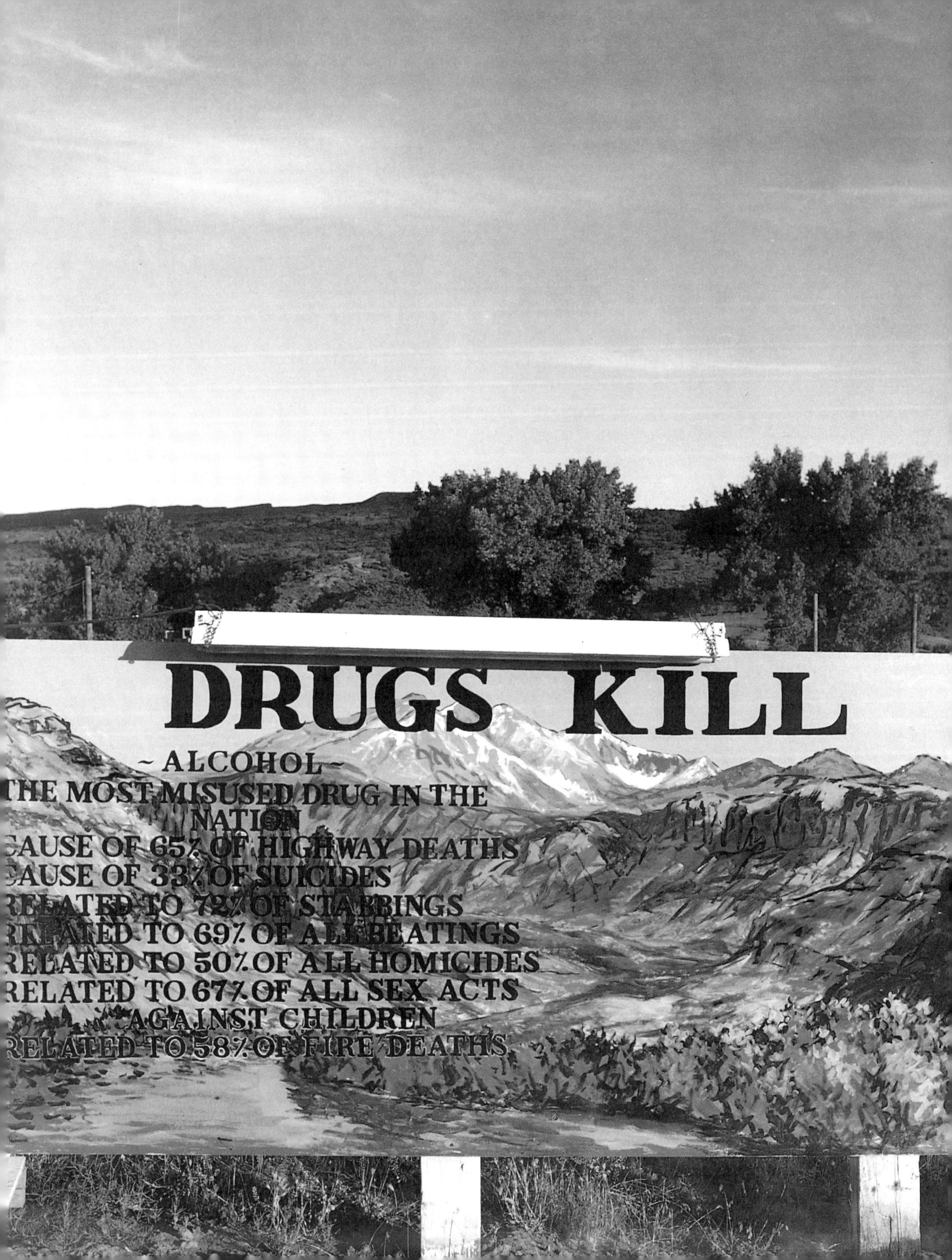
DRUGS KILL
~ALCOHOL~
THE MOST MISUSED DRUG IN THE
NATION
CAUSE OF 65% OF HIGHWAY DEATHS
CAUSE OF 33% OF SUICIDES
RELATED TO 72% OF STABBINGS
RELATED TO 69% OF ALL BEATINGS
RELATED TO 50% OF ALL HOMICIDES
RELATED TO 67% OF ALL SEX ACTS
AGAINST CHILDREN
RELATED TO 58% OF FIRE DEATHS

How to Use This Book

Substance Abuse is part of a six-volume encyclopedia series of books on health topics significant to junior-high students. These health topics are closely related to each other, and, for this reason, you'll see references to the other volumes in the series appearing throughout the book. You'll also see references to the other pages *within* this book. These references are important because they tell you where you can find more interrelated and interesting information on the specific subject at hand.

Like each of the books in the series, this book is divided into two sections. The first section tells you why it's a good idea for you to know about this health topic and how it affects you. The second section helps you find ways to improve and maintain your health. We include quizzes and plans designed to help you see how these health issues are related to you. It's your responsibility to take advantage of them and apply them to your life. Even though this book was written expressly for you and other people your age, you are the one who's in control of learning from it and exercising good health habits for the rest of your life.

PART I:

What's Important For Me To Know About Substance Abuse?

With very little effort, the average teenager learns something about substance abuse. Television shows you how people act when they've had too much alcohol. Friends tell you that cigarettes help them relax. Parents warn you that crack kills. In fact, it may seem like everyone older than you has tried drugs, cigarettes, or alcohol.

Yet, the kind of information you get from other people is sketchy and subjective; you probably have lots of unanswered questions, and you can't believe everything you hear. Society likes to "protect" teens from the facts, but as you'll read later, statistics point to substance abuse as a serious teen problem. The chances that tobacco, alcohol or illegal drugs won't cross your path are slim. The more informed you are, the better decisions you'll be able to make and the healthier you'll be.

The first part of this book deals with the facts: why teens participate in substance abuse; how alcohol, tobacco and drugs make you feel; the health problems these substances can cause; how people become addicted. Armed with this information, you'll be ready to go on to Part II, where you'll make certain decisions about substance abuse.

Fifteen to twenty-five percent of adults who began consuming alcohol as teenagers acknowledge they now have problems connected with its use.

Teenagers Are More Likely to be Risk Takers

What's a risk? Driving to school without a driver's license. Sneaking out of class without a pass. Walking through a dangerous part of town at night. Riding a motorcycle. Leaving your door unlocked.

There are different kinds of risks and everyone takes some. Business people generally thrive on risks, like investing money in ventures that may or may not pay off. You can probably think of examples at school that involve risk. Trying out for the basketball team is one; if you don't make the team, you risk disappointment. On the other hand, without taking the risk, you don't gain anything. Avoid every risk, and you'll never win a contest, sing a solo, or have a date for the dance.

Then there are health risks, like eating a high-fat diet, avoiding exercise, and letting stress get out of hand. Granted, we can't run away from every spoonful of sour cream or every stressful test. But it's safe to say that health risks are in the major leagues—they don't compare to other risks. But how do you benefit from taking another kind of health risk, such as smoking a cigarette? You may have your own reasons for taking risks but in practice, health risks really aren't so easily explained. (See "Nutrition"; "Exercise"; "Stress and Mental Health"; "Human Sexuality.")

Many young people want to experiment with alcohol and other drugs the same way they want to try other experiences. They don't believe that beer is dangerous just because their parents say so; they want to find out for themselves.

Why People Take Risks

Would you jump off a tall building? No. Although there's a small chance you'd avoid serious injury, you know the risk is very high. Plus, the consequences are immediate; after jumping off a tall building, you would be hurt on the spot, not three or four years from now.

Some health risks don't have the same immediate consequences. Doctors say that a high-fat diet can contribute to causing cancer, but you can eat french fries everyday for a whole week without getting cancer. In fact, it's possible to eat french fries everyday for the rest of your life without getting cancer. Doctors don't say that fatty foods cause cancer all of the time, but they do know that a high-fat diet increases the risk. Eating a high-fat diet, your chance of getting cancer someday might be three in ten; a low-fat diet, one in ten. (These aren't real risk percentages—just examples. Several factors, such as family history and exercise, also affect your risk.)

It's easy to see why someone would take a risk with long-term consequences rather than one with immediate consequences. It's one thing to pass up a drag race because the threat of injury is very real; it may be more difficult to resist a health risk when the injury or effect on your health is months or years away—and not even certain at that.

Tobacco, alcohol, and drugs possess this characteristic in common: When abused, they cause serious health problems, but not always immediately. In fact, on a short-term basis, these substances may be pleasurable for you. (Of course, drawing toxic smoke into your lungs isn't good for you physically, but some people think smoking a cigarette is very relaxing.)

© David M. Doody / FPG International

Family and peers set standards for young people. When parents or older brothers or sisters smoke, teenagers are likely to do the same. If you hang around with friends who like to smoke, you'll probably be tempted to do it yourself.

Why Teens Turn to Substance Abuse

Adults often ignore the long-term consequences of health risks; that is evident by the national statistics on heart disease and cancer. Teens do too, for many of the same reasons. For one, researchers say that most people tend to think more of the "here and now" and less about the future. Even adults are victims of this immature way of thinking, since they don't weigh all the pros and cons.

Just because this is "immature," it doesn't mean it's true of all young people. It just makes sense that a forty three-year-old person has more experience with life than a thirteen-year-old person, and therefore, is better able to judge most situations. This not only helps explain why teens drink alcohol or smoke crack, but also why they drive very fast or have sex before they're married. (See "Human Sexuality.")

Researchers also point out that teens go through a number of physical, emotional, and social changes in a very short period of time. As the body changes from that of a child's to an adult's, young people also find themselves in other phases of transition: They alternate between little-kid insecurity and a grown-up need for independence. At the same time, these changes create other emotional problems: Teens worry if they are normal, if they are popular, if they will be successful, and so on.

This need to be liked and accepted is the reason why young people depend on peer groups. As you probably know, teens are strongly influenced by their friends' appearance, dress, language, and free-time activities. By doing what a certain group of students do, you're usually more accepted than if you don't do what they do. If you want to fit in with a group of guys who all have very short hair, you might cut your own hair short. Or, if you want to be popular, and all the popular girls in your class wear mini-skirts, you'd wear mini-skirts rather than long skirts.

It makes sense, then, that if a group of students drink alcohol or try drugs, you or other teens might be drawn to these substances, too. Although doctors clearly define the health problems these substances cause, it's easy to ignore the long-term risks and focus on the present: peer pressure. (See "Human Sexuality.")

Perhaps you know people who smoke cigarettes, drink alcohol, or use drugs. Do they have reasons other than wanting to be part of a group. Are they thinking of the long-term consequences for trying these substances? There are many explanations for why people do these things or ignore the effects, and you'll read about them later. Even so, this basic theory of far-away health risks and peer pressure plays a part in most teen substance abuse cases.

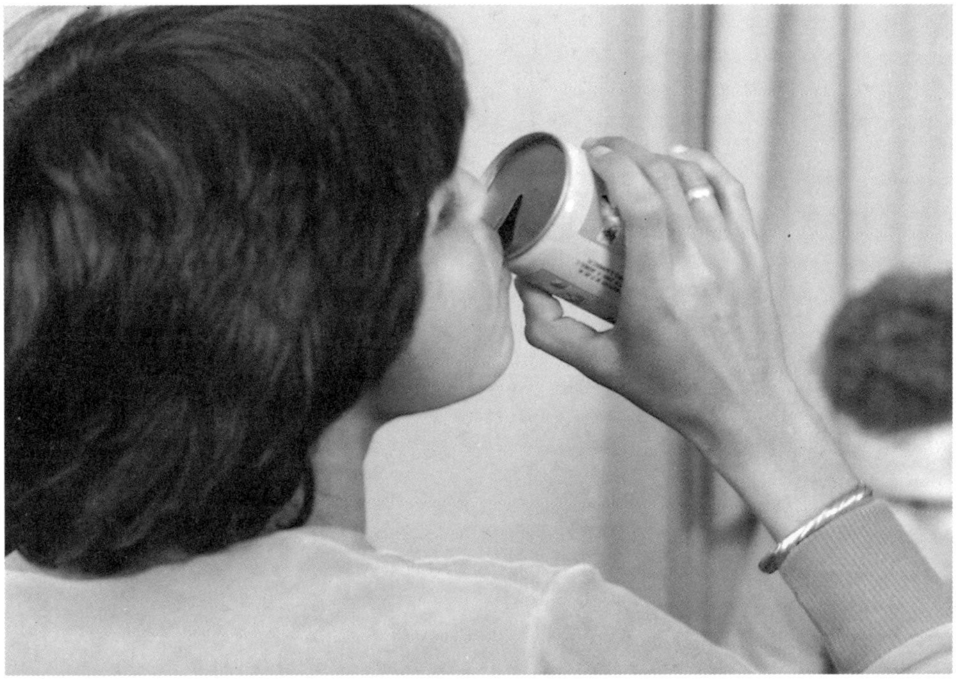

You can't make your parents or friends stop drinking, but you can try to help steer them in the healthiest direction. However, your decision to drink alcohol is all in your hands.

A lot of kids say they started using drugs because there was nothing better to do. Instead of drawing or painting, they do drugs.

© S. McCarroll/FPG International

A common definition of the word **drug**: *any substance that, in small amounts, produces changes in the body, mind, or both. Do you think the objects pictured here qualify?*

What is Substance Abuse?

A person's dependence on a substance isn't all in her head. The body becomes accustomed to the substance, so that if it is not present, the victim experiences withdrawal symptoms. To be addicted, a person isn't always physically dependent (although often, she is), but nevertheless feels a very strong mental need for the substance. The need is so strong that the person may think he's not able to function without it. This happens with tobacco, alcohol, and drugs.

You don't have to become addicted or physically dependent on a substance in order to abuse it. A person can abuse alcohol just by drinking beer and driving a car at the same time. People have died after experimenting with drugs for the first time. A person can smoke cigarettes without saying she's addicted, but she's still risking her health, and thus, abusing tobacco.

Actually, experts say *any* use of these substances by a teen is abuse. Why? The younger a person is when he develops an unhealthy habit, the greater his danger. First, the habit is stronger because he's devoted more time to it. Second, young people aren't fully grown, and an unhealthy lifestyle severely limits normal growth and development. Substances like drugs, tobacco, and alcohol interfere with normal development. Third, the health risks that *everyone* takes with these substances is more serious for people who started as teens; the longer you take health risks, the likelier the odds against good health are to catch up.

It's not that health experts want to make young people feel bad or scared; they're just concerned. Teens have enough changes to handle without having to juggle a drug or drinking problem.

Risk Quiz

Do you take any of the risks listed here? If so, write them on your own paper. Come up with at least ten risks, either from the ones we've listed here or any that you can think of on your own. Then, write the consequence(s) after each one. Is it an immediate or future consequence? Is it a positive or negative consequence? For each risk, draw a chart like the one below on your own paper and write in your risks the way we did.

RISK:	**Not doing my homework**	
	NEGATIVE	**POSITIVE**
IMMEDIATE	Getting a bad grade	Get to watch more TV
FUTURE	Fail 7th grade	

Not doing homework
Disobeying parents
Asking someone to a dance
Not wearing a seatbelt
Not bathing regularly
Skipping school
Driving without a license
Running for a school office
Not eating balanced meals
Not getting enough sleep
Not brushing and flossing teeth
Having sex
Trying to kiss a boy/girl
Wearing a new style of clothes to school
Trying out/auditioning for a team/ music or drama group
Driving above the speed limit
Joining a new club
Telephoning a boy or girl you like
Not exercising regularly
Smoking cigarettes
Drinking alcohol
Using drugs

Tobacco: Old Habits Die Hard

People used tobacco for 300 years before recognizing its harmful effects. Native Americans first grew the tobacco plant in order to smoke it during their ceremonies. When European explorers tried it, they spread the practice all over the world. For a while, only rich and highly educated people smoked tobacco, but eventually common men—and later, women—imitated the habit. Although some religious groups tried to outlaw tobacco use throughout the years, it wasn't until the 1900s that doctors made the health-and-tobacco connection: It can cause lung cancer, emphysema, heart disease, abnormal babies, and other disorders. (See pages 39–41.)

Tobacco may be smoked via a cigarette, cigar, or pipe; inhaled through the nose (called snuff); or chewed. But cigarettes are the preferred mode of nicotine intake in this country. According to statistics from the American Association for Cancer Research, about one-third of the nation's population smokes about 600 billion cigarettes a year. While fewer people smoked in 1984 than in 1964 (thirty percent compared to forty-two percent), today's smokers are smoking more cigarettes than they used to (593 billion per year, compared to 511 billion). The American Cancer Society estimates that one million teenagers and children in the United States start smoking every year.

TF True or False?

More teenage girls smoke than boys.

True. At one time, more males than females did smoke, but not now. Between 1968 and 1979, smoking among teenage boys decreased by thirty-six percent, but it *increased* among girls by some forty percent. About one-and-a-half times as many girls are smoking today as in 1968, and almost half of those girls smoke half a pack a day or more.

Why the increase? One theory points to advertisers: Since the 1950s, tobacco companies have developed attractive advertisements that show good-looking, sophisticated women with cigarettes. Women may be more influenced by these advertisments because they frequently appear in women's magazines. And women's magazines usually can't print bad news about smoking, since the publishers need the money that tobacco advertisers pay.

© Blumebild/FPG International

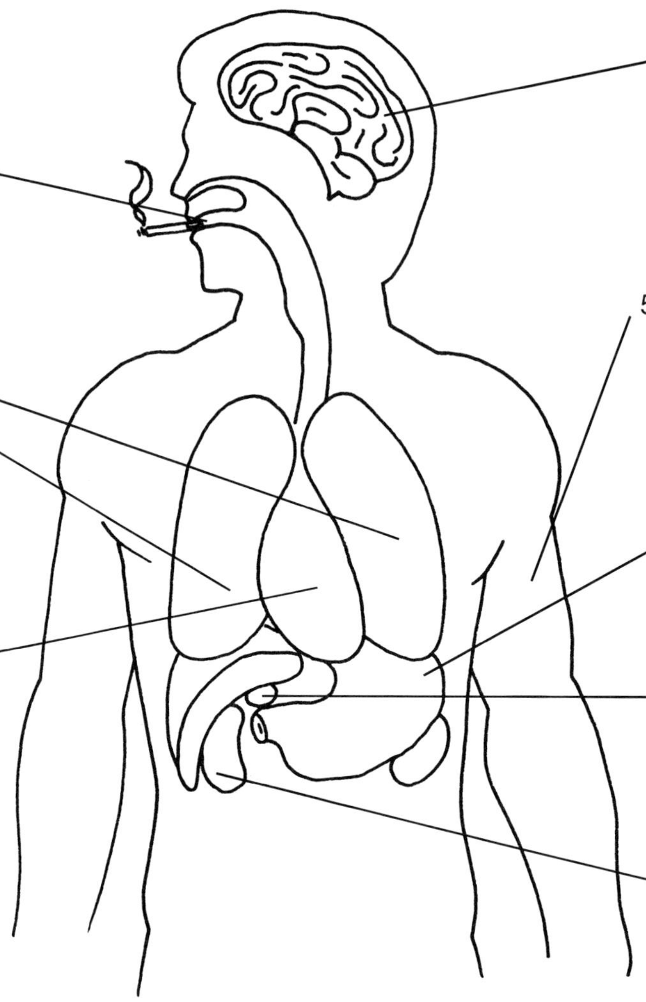

A Few Seconds with a Cigarette

Tobacco smoke is a mixture of about 3,000 chemical compounds, including gases, vapors, and small particles. (See "Smoke: What's in There?") In as little as seven seconds, these substances can travel all over the body for an almost instant effect:

1. The **mouth** helps you draw smoke into your windpipe and lungs. Consequently, the mouth and throat tissues may feel irritated.
2. The **lungs** deliver smoke to the bloodstream, which carries it to all parts of the body. At the same time, some of these smoke particles settle in the lung's tiny tubes.
3. The **brain** stimulates hormones that make you feel slightly stimulated or relaxed.
4. The **heart** rate increases.
5. **Blood vessels** constrict and the blood pressure rises.
6. The **stomach** is affected as hunger is depressed.
7. The **adrenal glands** make other mood-altering hormones.
8. Urine is inhibited when the **kidneys** come into contact with smoke substances.

Q. *Why is nicotine so addictive?*

A. Because it reaches the brain within seven seconds of taking a puff—faster than any other substance.

Q. *What's it like to smoke?*

A. People who smoke a lot complain of irritated eyes, sore throats, dulled tastebuds, hoarseness, coughing, shortness of breath, and a number of other things. Yet, they continue to smoke because they've smoked so much, they crave nicotine, the stimulant found in tobacco. (See "How Nicotine Becomes Addictive," page 28.) Basically, the first few puffs make smokers feel a little excited, stimulated, "up." Then, later into the cigarette or period of smoking, they feel more relaxed. This is because nicotine works on the brain and central nervous system, very complex parts of the body.

However, the beginning smoker often experiences symptoms of mild nicotine poisoning: dizziness, faintness, rapid pulse, cold, clammy skin—and sometimes nausea, vomiting, and diarrhea. Plus, most smokers will tell you they coughed and choked, their eyes watered and their throats hurt the first time they tried to smoke. Then again, some people think it's "cool" to ignore these discomforts, to cover up and pretend that smoking the first time feels better than it really does.

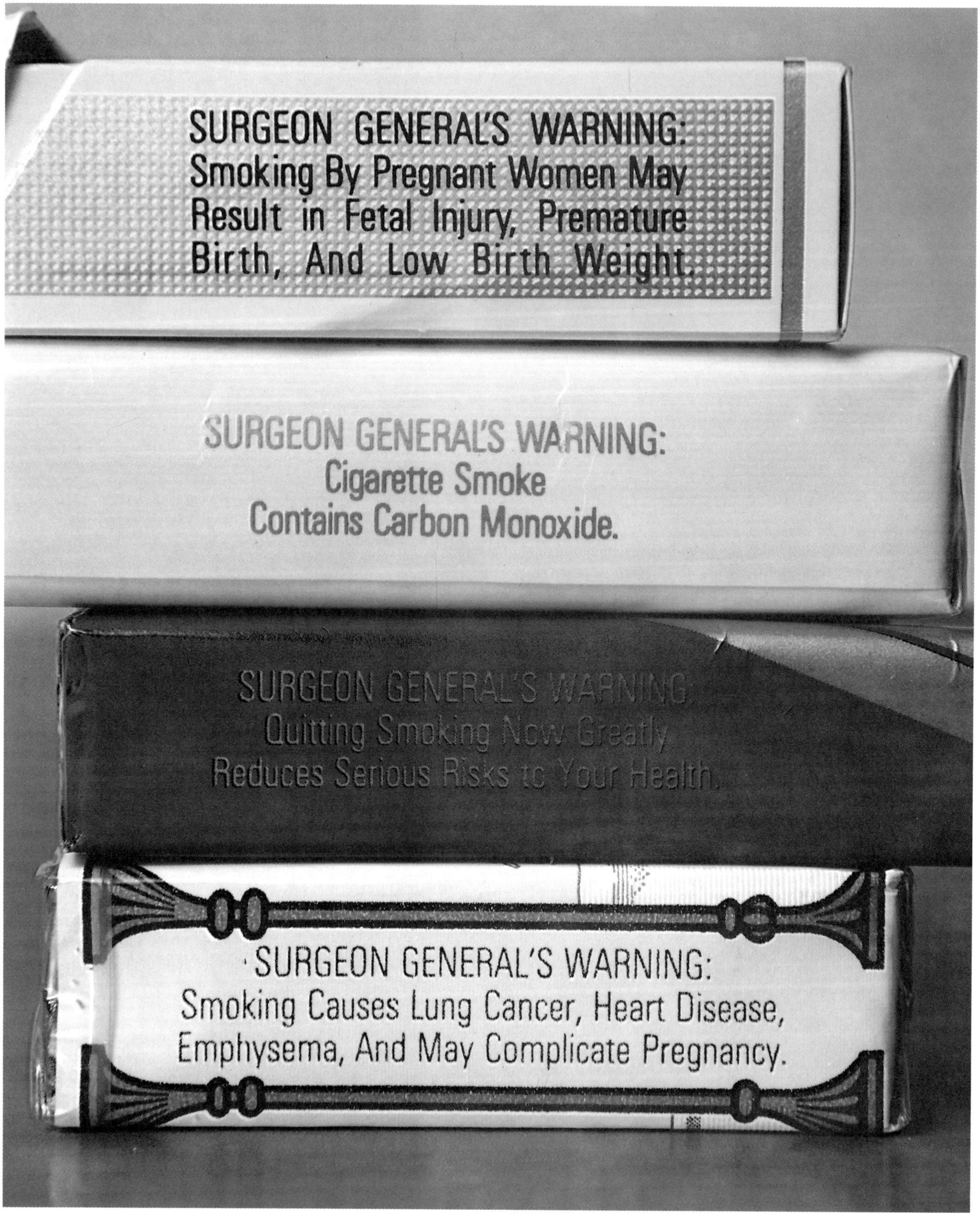
SURGEON GENERAL'S WARNING:
Smoking By Pregnant Women May Result in Fetal Injury, Premature Birth, And Low Birth Weight.
SURGEON GENERAL'S WARNING:
Cigarette Smoke Contains Carbon Monoxide.
SURGEON GENERAL'S WARNING:
Quitting Smoking Now Greatly Reduces Serious Risks to Your Health.
SURGEON GENERAL'S WARNING:
Smoking Causes Lung Cancer, Heart Disease, Emphysema, And May Complicate Pregnancy.

A pack-a-day smoker pours a cup of tar into his lungs each year.

Smoke: What's in There?

Tobacco smoke isn't just smoke: Scientists can break it down into thousands of chemicals and particles. Basically, however, most effects of tobacco smoke are related to three major components.

Nicotine, the colorless, oily chemical in tobacco, is responsible for cigarette addiction. It races from the lungs to the bloodstream to the brain in seconds to stimulate the heart and nervous system. When the body gets used to having a certain level of nicotine in the bloodstream, victims become physically dependent. Not only does this "drug" work on the brain, it also reduces the amount of blood carried to the heart, which eventually damages the heart tissues. Nicotine also affects the digestive system. (See "How Nicotine Becomes Addictive," page 28; "A Few Seconds with a Cigarette," page 22.)

Tar is the brownish, sticky stuff you see on ashtrays. Produced when tobacco is burned, tar is made of several hundred different chemicals, many of them carcinogens, which means they cause or help cause cancer. When smoke is inhaled, tar gets trapped in the lungs, and—just as it sticks to an ashtray—coats the respiratory (breathing) tract. This physical contact with tar promotes cancer. Tar can also damage the lungs' mucus (body fluid) and cilia (little hairlike structures) that help sweep out foreign materials.

Carbon monoxide is the same gas that comes out of a car's exhaust pipe. As you know, breathing these fumes can be fatal, so it makes sense that inhaling carbon monoxide in cigarette smoke is also dangerous. (Cigarette smokers have up to ten times as much carbon monoxide in their blood as nonsmokers.) When carbon monoxide enters the bloodstream from a cigarette, it prevents some of the blood cells from carrying oxygen to parts of the body. This is why smokers are often short of breath, their muscles hurt, and their endurance suffers during exercise. (See "Exercise.") Carbon monoxide also damages blood vessels and eyesight.

Q. *How does smoking affect breathing?*

A. When you breathe, your nose filters out about seventy-five percent of invisible foreign substances in the air. But when you smoke a cigarette, pipe, or cigar smoke goes directly through the mouth, the breathing tract, and the lungs. The nose gets passed up, and scores of harmful substances—even more than normal air has—get into the body.

TF True or False?

Cigarette smoke can cause wrinkles.

True. The compounds in tobacco smoke restrict your blood vessels, so your skin doesn't get a steady supply of blood. Years of smoking could result in wrinkles. Smoking can wrinkle your complexion in another way, too: Whenever you move your face muscles in a certain way for years and years, your skin may lose its elasticity and become creased. For example, if you frowned for the next five years, your forehead might become permanently wrinkled. In the same way, inhaling and exhaling cigarettes over several years can lead to puckered wrinkles around the mouth. A recent study showed that judges could pick the smokers out of groups of women just by looking at pictures of their faces.

Did You Know . . .

That nicotine is used as a weed killer? It's a poison. Sixty milligrams of nicotine taken at one time will kill that average adult human being by paralyzing breathing. The reason it doesn't kill smokers quickly is that they inhale tiny doses (a cigarette has between 0.5 and 2 milligrams), which are quickly used or disposed of by the body.

How Nicotine Becomes Addictive

When a person first begins to smoke, he may get only a little pleasure from it. Smoking can irritate the mouth, throat, eyes; leave a "stale" smell on one's breath and clothes; stain the teeth; leave a bad taste in the mouth; and cause coughing. As you read in "What's It Like to Smoke,?" page 23, one might also experience mild nicotine poisoning.

Eventually, the smoker develops an addiction to nicotine. It's true that the smoker may pick up cigarettes as a force of habit—just as you might twist your hair or bite your fingernails by habit. Psychologically, smokers get used to having a cigarette in their hands and putting it to their mouths for a puff. But to be physically dependent is not just a matter of having something to hold or put in your mouth. Instead, the body craves the nicotine and makes the smoker feel uncomfortable when he doesn't get it. You could liken the sensation to that of a drug addict who can't get the drug he needs, or an alcoholic who needs her drink to feel good.

How does one develop a dependence on nicotine? When nicotine makes contact with the brain, it stimulates certain areas, which sets off several changes in the body. (See "A Few Seconds with a Cigarette," page 22.) It's as if nicotine pushes "pleasure buttons" in the brain. In time, the body gets used to having a certain level of nicotine; if it doesn't get that level, those pleasure buttons don't get pushed. The result: withdrawal symptoms, such as irritability, anxiety, craving—generally, very bad moods. If you've ever watched someone try to stop smoking, you know this is true. Of course, if the smoker waits long enough, the body gets used to living without nicotine, and in fact, feels better.

Doctors know that nicotine is the chief troublemaker. Do you know heavy smokers? Have you ever noticed how they will smoke several cigarettes in the morning? This is called "loading"; because the smokers have not smoked since they went to bed, they have to get the nicotine in their bloodstreams up to a comfortable level. Throughout the day, they'll smoke enough cigarettes to maintain that high.

In one study, researchers gave cigarettes with different levels of nicotine to their subjects. Some had as little as 0.5 milligrams per cigarette; others four times as much, 2.0 milligrams. Interestingly, the subjects adjusted the number of cigarettes they smoked to suit the level of nicotine they found most comfortable in their bodies. If they were smoking low-nicotine cigarettes, they smoked more: If they were smoking cigarettes high in nicotine, they smoked fewer than usual. They also puffed differently; by inhaling more deeply, a smoker gets a more concentrated dose of nicotine. Short, little puffs deliver low doses of nicotine to the bloodstream.

Smokers are telling the truth when they say it's hard to quit. If they have been smoking long enough, they really do depend on nicotine.

Q. If nicotine and tar are so bad, then why don't people just switch to "light" cigarettes?

A. They do, and studies show that lung cancer cases decreased with the coming of this new breed of cigarettes in which tar and nicotine levels were cut in half. However, when smokers are addicted to nicotine, they may unconsciously adjust their smoking habits in order to maintain a certain level of nicotine in the body. If they smoke light cigarettes, they smoke more cigarettes, inhale more deeply, and smoke all the way to the butt. In the end, they defeat the purpose of light cigarettes.

TAR AND NICOTINE LEVELS IN CIGARETTES

Here is a sampling of the tar and nicotine levels in certain brands of cigarettes, according to the latest tests done by the Federal Trade Commission. These figures will give you an idea of the amounts of tar and nicotine in each cigarette, though questions have been raised—by the cigarette manufacturers mostly—about the accuracy of the results. On the other hand, tests also show that a person who smokes a cigarette lower in tar usually smokes more cigarettes!

BRAND	TYPE	TAR (mg/cig)	NICOTINE (mg/cig)
Now 100's	100 mm, filter (hardpack)	0.5	0.05
Carlton 100's	100 mm, filter, menthol (hardpack)	0.5	0.01
Benson & Hedges	reg. size, filter (hardpack)	1	0.1
Kool Ultra	king size, filter, menthol	2	0.2
Lucky 100's	100 mm, filter	3	0.3
Merit Ultra Lights	king size, filter, menthol	3	0.3
Winston Ultra	king size, filter	4	0.4
Pall Mall Extra Light	king size, filter	6	0.6
Camel Lights	king size, filter, (hardpack)	8	0.7
Virginia Slims Lights 100's	100 mm, filter, (hardpack)	9	0.7
Kool Super Lights 100's	100 mm, filter, menthol	9	0.7
Marlboro Lights	king size, filter	11	0.8
Eve Lights 100's	100 mm, filter	13	1.0
Marlboro	king size, filter, menthol	15	0.9
Salem	king size, filter, menthol	15	1.0
Virginia Slims 100's	100 mm, filter	15	1.0
Marlboro 100's	100 mm, filter	17	1.1
Camel	reg. size, non-filter	20	1.3
Players	reg. size, non-filter, (hardpack)	25	1.8

Measure Your Nicotine Dependence

Give this quiz to someone you know who smokes: your boyfriend, mother, brother, teacher, even yourself.

1. How soon after you wake up do you smoke your first cigarette?

A. Almost right away
B. Between thirty minutes to an hour
C. More than an hour later

2. How difficult is it to not smoke when you first wake up?

A. Very difficult
B. Somewhat difficult
C. Not at all

3. How difficult is to not smoke in places where it's not allowed, such as theaters, church, school, etc.?

A. Very difficult
B. Somewhat difficult
C. Not at all

4. How often do you find yourself hurrying to smoke after you haven't been able to?

A. Almost always
B. Sometimes
C. Almost never

5. Do you enjoy smoking at the end of the day?

A. Very much
B. Somewhat
C. Not at all

6. How hard is it to keep from smoking when you're under pressure such as studying for tests or waiting for someone important to call?

A. Very difficult
B. Somewhat difficult
C. Not at all

7. How often do you smoke while relaxing?

A. Almost always
B. Sometimes
C. Almost never

8. How often do you smoke when you're upset or mad?

A. Almost always
B. Sometimes
C. Almost never

9. How much do you enjoy smoking around other smokers?

A. Very much
B. Somewhat
C. Not at all

10. How hard is it to not smoke when around other smokers?

A. Very difficult
B. Somewhat difficult
C. Not at all

11. How often do you smoke when you're around other smokers?

A. Almost always
B. Sometimes
C. Almost never

Scoring
A = 3 points; B = 2 points; C = 1 point.

1. Add up your scores for questions 1 through 4. 10–12 points: high dependence on nicotine. 7–9 points: moderate dependence on nicotine. 4–6 points: low dependence on nicotine.

2. Add up your scores for questions 5 through 8. 10–12 points: Cigarettes help you handle stress. 7–9 points: Cigarettes sometimes help you deal with stress. 4–6 points: You don't smoke to handle stress, but for other reasons.

3. Add up your scores for questions 9 through 11. 8–9 points: You are influenced by the smokers around you. 6–7 points: You're somewhat tempted by those around you. 3–5: Other smokers have little effect on you. You smoke for other reasons.

This quiz isn't designed to solve or completely analyze your smoking problem, but to help you begin to determine your level of dependence and where your problem areas are. While no level of smoking is safe, smokers with moderate or high scores will especially appreciate the helpful information in Part II. If your problem area is fellow smokers, be sure to read "Peer Pressure," page 101.

Q. Why Teens Say They Smoke

Reasons Teens Give for Smoking

- Because their friends do
- Because smoking looks sophisticated or cool
- Because they don't know its health risk
- Because a role model (parents, brother, sister, etc.) smokes
- Because they want to rebel against parents, teachers, etc.
- Because they're curious
- Because it helps them relax
- Because it makes them feel older

Reasons Teens Give for Not *Smoking*

- Because it's dangerous to their health
- Because it makes hair, clothes, and breath smell bad
- Because it stains teeth and fingers a yellowish-brown color
- Because it costs a lot of money
- Because it makes other people mad
- Because it hinders breathing during exercise
- Because their parents don't want them to
- Because it dulls the senses of taste and smell

Q. Do cigarettes help you lose weight?

A. Smokers don't feel as hungry as nonsmokers. Not only does smoking affect the appetite by stimulating certain hormones in the brain, it also dulls the tastebuds, so food doesn't taste as good. This helps explain why some people gain weight when they stop smoking. Not only does food taste better, new nonsmokers often reach for food because they can't reach for a cigarette.

Unfortunately, some smokers—especially women—use weight gain as an excuse for not stopping. Even though smart eating habits would prevent an unhealthy weight gain, they would rather take the health risk that smoking poses.

You Really Want a Cigarette . . .

So Do One of These Things Instead:

- Take a walk
- Go for a jog
- Take a bubble bath
- Brush your teeth and use mouthwash
- Eat something healthy and low calorie, like a carrot
- Drink water—try one of the fancy fizzy kinds—or juice
- Chew a piece of sugarless gum
- Play the piano—or just pound on the keys
- Build something
- Hit a tennis ball against the garage door

SMOKING

	NEGATIVE	POSITIVE
SHORT-TERM CONSEQUENCES	• Expensive • Bad breath, smelly hair and clothes • Stained teeth and fingers • Shortness of breath • Coughing, hoarseness • Bad taste in mouth, less ability to taste food • More frequent illnesses and fatigue • Problems with nonsmokers who don't like smoke	• Stimulates, improves mental ability • Relaxes, calms • Dampens hunger • Makes you feel older, sophisticated • Helps you get "accepted"
LONG-TERM CONSEQUENCES	• Cancer of the mouth • Cancer of the esophagus • Cancer of the larynx • Lung cancer • Bladder cancer • Heart disease • Lung diseases (bronchitis, emphysema) • Ulcers • Circulatory diseases	

Short-Term Gains vs. Long-Term Losses

After reading "Teenagers Are More Likely to Be Risk Takers" (page 13) and seeing the chart, you can see the positive consequences of smoking are mainly short-term. Although there are some short-term factors most people wouldn't consider to be good about smoking—such as bad breath and coughing—smokers are usually convinced that the good outweighs the bad. For example, teens might shrug off the expense of buying cigarettes because they think it's important to be like their smoking friends. Plus, they only buy one pack at a time, which doesn't seem to be a lot of money.

Yet, after looking at the long-term risks, the short-term gains pale in comparison. About twenty years ago, the Surgeon General reported that cigarette smoking is the major single cause of cancer mortality (death) in the United States. The American Heart Association estimates that about one-fourth of all fatal heart attacks in the United States are caused by cigarette smoking—about 120,000 heart attack deaths per year. And there are plenty more statistics like these.

Lung Cancer: A cigarette smoker is over ten times more likely to develop lung cancer than a nonsmoker. When smoke is inhaled, tar deposits get trapped in the lungs. This foreign substance damages the tissues, possibly causing abnormal growth of cells.

The chances of curing lung cancer are very low; once it's diagnosed, only one out of ten people live more than five years. Unfortunately, the symptoms of lung cancer (persistent cough, chest pain, frequent bronchitis and pneumonia attacks, coughed-up blood) don't usually show up until the disease is fairly advanced. But if smokers stop smoking before cancer has started, their lung tissue tends to repair itself. Evidence shows that one year after a person stops smoking, the risk of lung cancer decreases steadily, almost to nonsmoker levels.

Q. Why do smokers have a "cigarette cough"?

A. When a person puffs on a cigarette, substances from the smoke irritate the air passages and lungs. It's their job to push out foreign matter, and they do that by making you cough.

But when a smoker coughs during the early morning, that's usually due to something else. When smoke is drawn into the lungs, it "deadens" the cilia, tiny hairlike structures lining the airways that normally force foreign matter from the lungs. When they stop working, some of the substances stay in the lungs. But when a smoker is sleeping and not smoking, the cilia "come back to life." When the smoker gets up, he begins to cough, because his lungs are trying to clear out the previous day's smoke deposits.

Unfortunately, when cilia are repeatedly exposed to smoke over a long period of time, they lose their ability to work at all. This puts a smoker's lung at even more risk of disease.

Facts About Teens and Smoking

- Each day, 4,000 American young people try smoking for the first time.
- If a parent or older brother or sister smokes, a teen is four times more likely to smoke than if no one in the family smokes cigarettes.
- Junior-high students whose schools are attached to a senior-high school are more likely to smoke.
- A teenager with a lot of friends and high self-esteem is more likely to avoid smoking, even when he or she has pressure to try it.

Heart Disease: Smokers have a seventy percent higher death rate from heart disease than nonsmokers; heavy smokers have a 200 percent higher death rate. Scientists know that nicotine raises the heart rate and blood pressure and constricts blood vessels because the carbon monoxide from cigarettes decreases the amount of oxygen delivered to the heart. This means the heart has to work even harder on reduced fuel. If something blocks an aorta (major blood vessel) and blood can't get to the heart, a person may have a heart attack. If blood can't get to the brain, a stroke may occur. Other heart disorders have been linked to smoking, but these are the most dangerous. (See "Nutrition.")

Other Cancers: Besides lung cancer, smoking is also associated with cancer of the mouth, throat, larynx (voicebox), and esophagus (the tube from the mouth to the stomach). Smoking increases the risk of mouth and throat cancers four to fifteen times, depending on the amount and type of tobacco used. Along with pipe and cigar smoking, tobacco chewing and snuff dipping (placing a wad of snuff into the mouth against the gums) increase the risk of cancers of the mouth and throat.

Fifty to seventy percent of the deaths from cancer of the mouth or larynx are attributed to smoking while fifty percent of cancer of the esophagus deaths are caused by smoking. Pipe smoking has been identified as a cause of lip cancer, and people who both smoke and drink alcohol run a greater risk of mouth or throat cancer than do those who use only one of the drugs. People as young as fifteen have died from mouth cancer caused by chewing tobacco.

Apparently, the dangerous matter that smoking introduces to the body can affect more than the direct-contact body parts, such as the mouth and lungs. Thirty to forty percent of bladder and kidney cancer cases are related to smoking. In addition, smoking has been linked to other cancers of the respiratory and digestive systems as well as to cancer of the stomach, pancreas, and cervix.

Andy Was Afraid of Smoking

His grandfather had died of a heart attack and the doctor said his death was related to his smoking cigarettes. So it didn't really bother Andy to tell people he didn't want to smoke. Besides, most of his friends were on the baseball team, and they preferred chewing tobacco. Andy figured that chewing tobacco was safer than smoking. He had *never heard of anyone dying from an occasional plug.*

You've probably heard other people justify the use of smokeless tobacco this way. In fact, health authorities are worried because the production of United States chewing tobacco increased fifty percent between 1971 and 1981. In different studies around the country, as many as one third of high-school students used smokeless tobacco.

But as you might have guessed, smokeless tobacco isn't safe either. People who chew tobacco and dip snuff can also become addicted to nicotine. The risk of cheek and gum cancers increases by nearly fifty times in long-term users of snuff or chewing tobacco. Smokeless tobacco comes into repeated, direct, prolonged contact with the mouth and teeth, causing the gums to recede, the teeth to become discolored and loose, and the biting surfaces to wear away.

Another risk for teens who use smokeless tobacco: As they get older, chewing tobacco and dipping snuff is anything but sophisticated. Most people think it's an ugly habit. Already addicted to nicotine, tobacco chewers switch to cigarettes to feed their addiction.

Respiratory Diseases: Emphysema and chronic bronchitis are two major diseases associated with smoking. In emphysema, the walls of the lungs' air sacs are gradually destroyed, so it's difficult for the victim to inhale and exhale. Consequently, an emphysema patient is frequently breathless, and the heart has to work harder in order to get oxygen. Death from a damaged heart sometimes occurs.

In chronic bronchitis, the bronchial tubes in the lungs become inflamed and excess mucus is produced. This causes the victim to cough a lot, which makes breathing difficult. Smokers are about eighteen times more likely to die from emphysema or bronchitis than nonsmokers. At the same time, smokers with bronchitis face a greater risk of lung cancer, no matter how old they are or how many cigarettes they smoke.

The risk of pregnancy problems or abnormal babies is *even higher* for teenage mothers, since they are more likely than adult mothers to have complications—even when they don't smoke. (See "Human Sexuality.")

The latest research points to negative consequences from the father's smoking. Although there's no evidence that the father's smoking hurts the fetus (unborn baby), smoking can slow the father's ability to help create one. Some studies show increasing levels of smoking are associated with a higher number of abnormal sperm. That's why doctors recommend that both would-be parents give up smoking before conceiving (fertilizing a female egg with a male sperm). (See "Human Sexuality.")

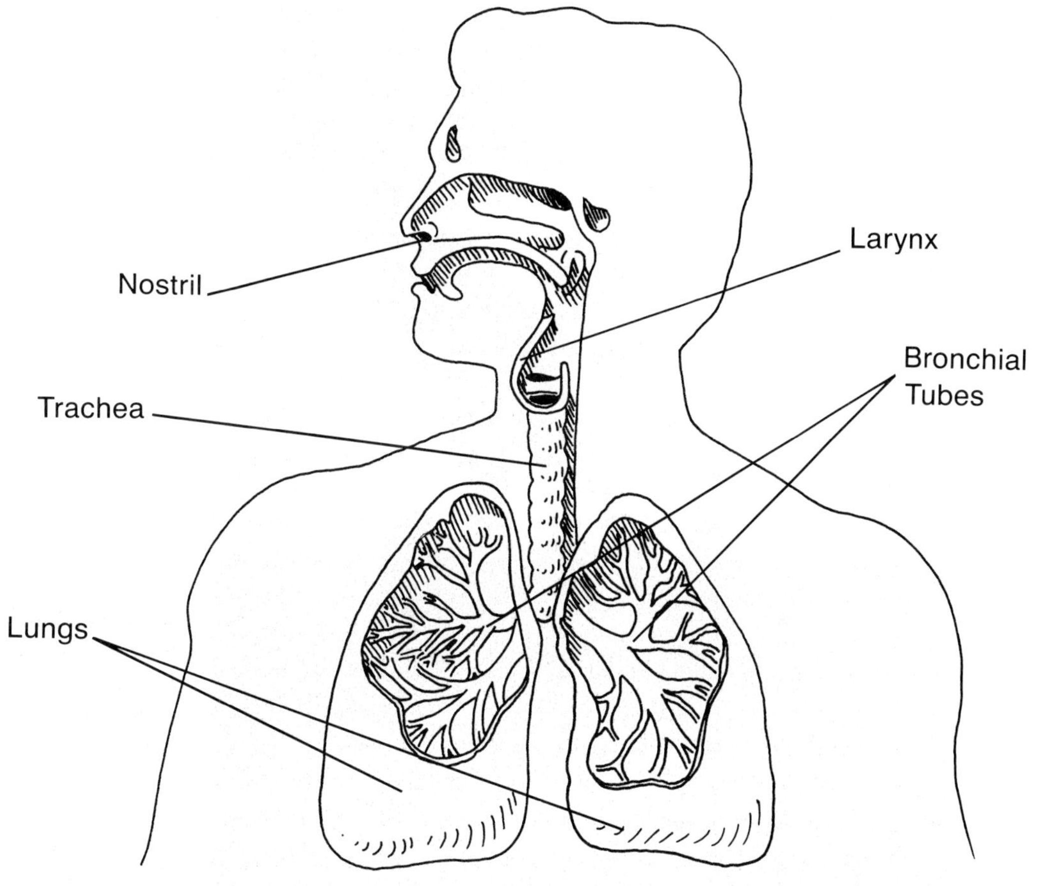

Q. Does air pollution cause lung cancer or respiratory diseases?

A. Maybe. In industrial areas or cities heavily polluted with smog, lung cancer rates are slightly higher than in rural areas. However, in both places, the lung cancer and disease rates are always much higher among smokers than nonsmokers. Although air pollution could cause these problems by itself, it's clear that people who smoke *and* live in polluted areas or work where there's lots of radioactive dust or other carcinogens (cancerous materials) have an even higher risk of getting sick.

© Peter Gridley/FPG International

Have you heard of environmental carcinogens? Simply put, these are natural or manufactured substances that could cause cancer. These substances range from coal tar to uranium to any of the various chemical agents found in air pollution.

Up in Smoke: Burning Accidents

Perhaps you've heard that old safety rule, "Never smoke in bed," or the public service slogan, "Only *you* can prevent forest fires." Maybe you've heard them so many times, you kind of ignore them. A lot of people do. But if you watch or listen to the news, you know that many house fires are started when someone falls asleep with a lighted cigarette, or that fires wiping out acres of land were probably due to a cigarette butt that didn't get stubbed out. In fact, in 1981, an estimated 2,000 Americans lost their lives and more than 3,000 others were injured in cigarette-related fires. So those rules may be oldies, but they're also goodies.

Pregnancy: In recent years, there has been increasing evidence that women who smoke during pregnancy put their babies' health and lives at risk. Experts say smoking increases blood levels of carbon monoxide, which prevents the unborn baby from getting enough oxygen. The result: Not only might the baby of a smoker be born at a below-normal weight (which means he is more likely to get sick or die before he grows up), he is also more likely to be born prematurely, or with heart or respiratory problems. Also, since the brain needs oxygen to develop, a mother's smoking may affect her unborn baby's intellectual development. Unfortunately, smoking during pregnancy also increases the risk of miscarriage (when the baby is born before it's old enough or strong enough to survive) or stillbirth (when the baby is born dead).

Other Health Hazards: The list is long and maybe even boring, but the health problems caused by smoking go beyond what you've already read. Cigarette smoke is composed of a huge number of different substances and researchers believe they affect a great many parts of the body. (See "Smoke: What's in There?", page 25.)

For one thing, people who smoke are more likely to have and die from ulcers or other disorders of the stomach. Tobacco use has also been linked with cirrhosis (a liver disease) and may aggravate disorders such as diabetes and hypertension (high blood pressure).

What's more, all kinds of statistics have been compiled about smoking and illnesses. Examples:

- Smokers spend one-third more days away from their jobs than nonsmokers. This means if the average worker spends about ten days at home sick, the smoking worker is out three to four more days.
- Women smokers spend seventeen percent more days sick in bed than women nonsmokers.
- A boy who takes up smoking before age fifteen and continues to smoke is only half as likely to live to age seventy-five as a boy who never smokes.

Why is this true? Besides causing the harmful effects already described, tobacco also harms the immune systems of people. When the immune system doesn't work, people's bodies aren't as strong when fighting off sickness, which is what they have to do all the time. Otherwise, we would never survive all the germs and foreign substances in our environments.

Q. *If cigarettes are so bad, then why don't all smokers get sick and die?*

A. You've probably heard of the ninety-year-old grandfatherly types who claim they smoked every day of their lives since they were fifteen, and are still as "fit as a fiddle." There are plenty of celebrities who have also defeated the odds. In fact, not too long ago, a great actor named Jackie Gleason was very well known for his high-risk lifestyle. He smoked cigars and drank alcohol and refused to stop, even though he was overweight, had diabetes, and was in his seventies. It seemed as if his risk-taking would never catch up with him, until 1987. Doctors then told him he had cancer. Did he stop smoking? No, but he died shortly thereafter.

There will always be people who will not appear to be affected by taking health risks. People react differently to all substances for a variety of reasons, including family history, individual biological makeup, and other lifestyle habits. For example, a smoker with heart disease in his family is more likely to suffer from this problem than a smoker who doesn't. A smoker who eats a high-fat diet is more likely to get cancer than a smoker who eats healthfully. (See "Nutrition.")

Even though there are people who have been lucky to avoid illness in spite of their health risks, it's possible the same thing that happened to Jackie Gleason could happen to them. True, Jackie Gleason lived until his seventies, but who knows how long he might have lived if he had exercised a healthful lifestyle? Taking risks is like playing Russian roulette—you may be the lucky one or you may not, but someone will pay the price. This is why life-insurance companies charge less money for nonsmokers and more money for smokers.

Passive Smoking

Cigarettes have a bad enough reputation for smokers, and now research is coming out about passive smoking. When you inhale the smoke of others, you are passive smoking. In other words, if you can smell another person's smoke, you are inhaling some of the same toxins the smoker inhales.

How dangerous is it? More than you might think. Smoke from someone else's cigar, cigarette, or pipe has two times more nicotine, five times as much carbon monoxide, and forty-six times as much ammonia as the smoke inhaled directly from them. Smoke in the air isn't filtered by the remaining tobacco in the cigarette; when a person draws on a cigarette, the tobacco in the cigarette screens out some of the harmful burning substances. (This is why smoking all the way down to the butt is more harmful. There is no tobacco to filter the smoke.) Passive smokers get the brunt of the smoke from another person's cigarettes. One study shows that nonsmoking wives of smoking men died an average of four years earlier than those whose husbands did not smoke. Children in households where one or both parents smoke have double the amount of bronchitis or pneumonia during the first year of life as children in nonsmoking households.

With studies like these in the news, it's easy to see why more and more people object to smokers in public places. Some states have already passed laws that limit where people can smoke, and many more states are trying to institute laws like them. Although it's not likely that smoking will be completely banned in the near future, there may soon be a time when smoking is only allowed outdoors.

© Daniella Nilva

Come to Marlboro Country and Dare to be More

Even if you don't smoke, it's likely that you know a few slogans from cigarette advertising campaigns. We see them in print media, such as newspapers, magazines, and billboards, but before 1971, cigarette advertisements also appeared on television and radio. Since then, the tobacco industry has been limited somewhat in their advertising, but even so, they spend over twenty-four billion dollars per year to sell their products.

Whether we realize it or not, advertising has an effect on us. In one recent study, pictures of the same female model was shown to teenage girls. All of the pictures were identical except that in one picture, the model was holding a cigarette. Interestingly, the teens rated the image of the model with the cigarette as more intelligent, more sophisticated, and healthier than those pictures without the cigarette.

In a way, it's easy to see why. Tobacco advertisers usually show models who are healthy and good-looking, doing the things we all like to do: playing tennis, riding in sports cars, dancing, or skiing. The models always look happy, sophisticated, and glamorous, and they are usually doing things that have nothing to do with smoking.

Even as advertisers pour on the charm, other groups are fighting to further restrict tobacco ads. All cigarette packages and ads are required to carry the words "Warning: The Surgeon General Has Determined That Cigarette Smoking Is Dangerous to Your Health." Editors are struggling with the fact that allowing the tobacco industry to place ads in their magazines makes them look bad, especially if they also feature health news. While there's no denying that people who work in the tobacco industry have a lot of influence in the United States government, they are sure to meet even more opposition in the future.

Q. *How much do cigarette manufacturers earn?*

A. If a cigarette advertisement can get one teenager to take up smoking for good, the industry earns about $25,000 to $30,000 during the lifetime of that person. That's a lot of cigarettes and a lot of money for just one smoker!

Something to Do

Go through an old magazine and look for cigarette and alcohol ads. Cut out the pictures from the ads, but leave out the products: the cigarettes or alcohol. Also cut out any words that mention the tobacco or alcohol product (such as "cigarettes" or "beer" or "wine"), the product's name (such as "Light" or "Cool"), and any writing about the product.

Now take a good look. How much do the pictures have to do with cigarettes and alcohol? Why do you think advertisers created this image to go with their product? Do you think you have to smoke or drink to be as happy as the people in the picture?

Alcohol: A Blast from the Past

What is probably the oldest drug in the world? The drink that was used around 5000 B.C. and maybe even earlier: alcohol. Scientists have found evidence from this time period that shows the ancient Babylonians were familiar with beer. In fact, they considered it a gift from the gods and brewed it as part of their religious ceremonies. Throughout history, alcohol has played some starring roles. At times, it's been used as a medicine. Other times, it's been criticized and outlawed.

To this day, few of us are strangers to alcohol, a substance that is legal and believed to be the most widely used drug in America. There's little doubt that drinking is one of our society's favorite pastimes. Unless it's against a group's values—whether family, ethnic, or religious—alcohol is featured at all kinds of gatherings: graduations, weddings, ball games, dinner parties, business meetings, even funerals.

The most used drug, alcohol is also said to be America's most abused. According to the Department of Health and Human Services, two-thirds of the country's population drink—and they drink heartily, enough for *every person* in the country to have 591 cans of beer, 115 bottles of wine, or thirty-five fifths of whisky a year. This doesn't mean that all people who drink alcohol abuse it or are alcoholics. Plenty of people know how to drink wisely, but too many don't. The National Institute on Alcohol Abuse and Alcoholism (NIAAA) estimates that one in ten Americans who drink is an alcoholic. Alcohol-related cirrhosis (a liver disease) is the sixth leading cause of death in the United States, and one-half of all traffic fatalities (deaths) are associated with alcohol use.

Young people are also getting into the act. The NIAAA now says the average kid takes his first drink at around age thirteen, but as many as forty percent of young people have their first drink by the age of ten. If this is true, you should know what alcohol is, what happens when it passes through your body, and what the long-term consequences are.

Defining a Drink

Alcohol is made by either fermentation or distillation. Beer and wine are fermented products; they're made when certain yeasts are allowed to act on the sugars found in fruit and grain. Liquors like whisky, gin, and rum are made by distillation, which is a process involving cooking.

However these drinks are prepared, they all contain ethyl alcohol. Depending on the kind of drink, ethyl alcohol (people usually just shorten it to "alcohol") comes in different amounts. Wines contain from eight to sixteen percent alcohol; beer, three to nine percent; distilled liquors, forty to fifty percent.

The best way to gauge alcohol content is to follow this easy rule. A twelve-ounce can of beer, a five-ounce glass of wine, and a one-and-a-half ounce shot of liquor (which is usually in a cocktail drink) all have about the same amount of alcohol—0.6 ounces. Remember: A drink is a drink is a drink—no matter what it is.

The Proof Isn't Always on the Label

How can you tell how much alcohol a bottle of beer or wine has? Liquor's alcohol content is measured in proof, which is twice the percentage of alcohol by volume. In other words, a bottle of liquor that's eighty proof is forty percent alcohol.

The alcohol content of wine is shown by volume. Since the average bottle of wine is eleven percent alcohol by volume, you know it's also twenty-two proof.

Beer labels, on the other hand, don't show the amount of alcohol they contain. But most beer is four-and-a-half percent alcohol by volume, or nine proof.

TF True or False?

Alcohol is in perfume.

True. But it's not the same as ethyl alcohol, which is what we drink. Alcohol can be found in cleaning solutions, ink, varnish, paint thinner, and other products. They contain methyl alcohol, which is toxic and should *never be consumed.* Alcohol is a general term that is used for a group of chemical substances.

A drink is a drink is a drink. In other words, the alcohol content of a 12-ounce bottle or can of beer, a five-ounce glass of wine, and a one-and-a-half ounce shot of whiskey is about the same. A six pack has the same alcohol content as six glasses of wine or six shots.

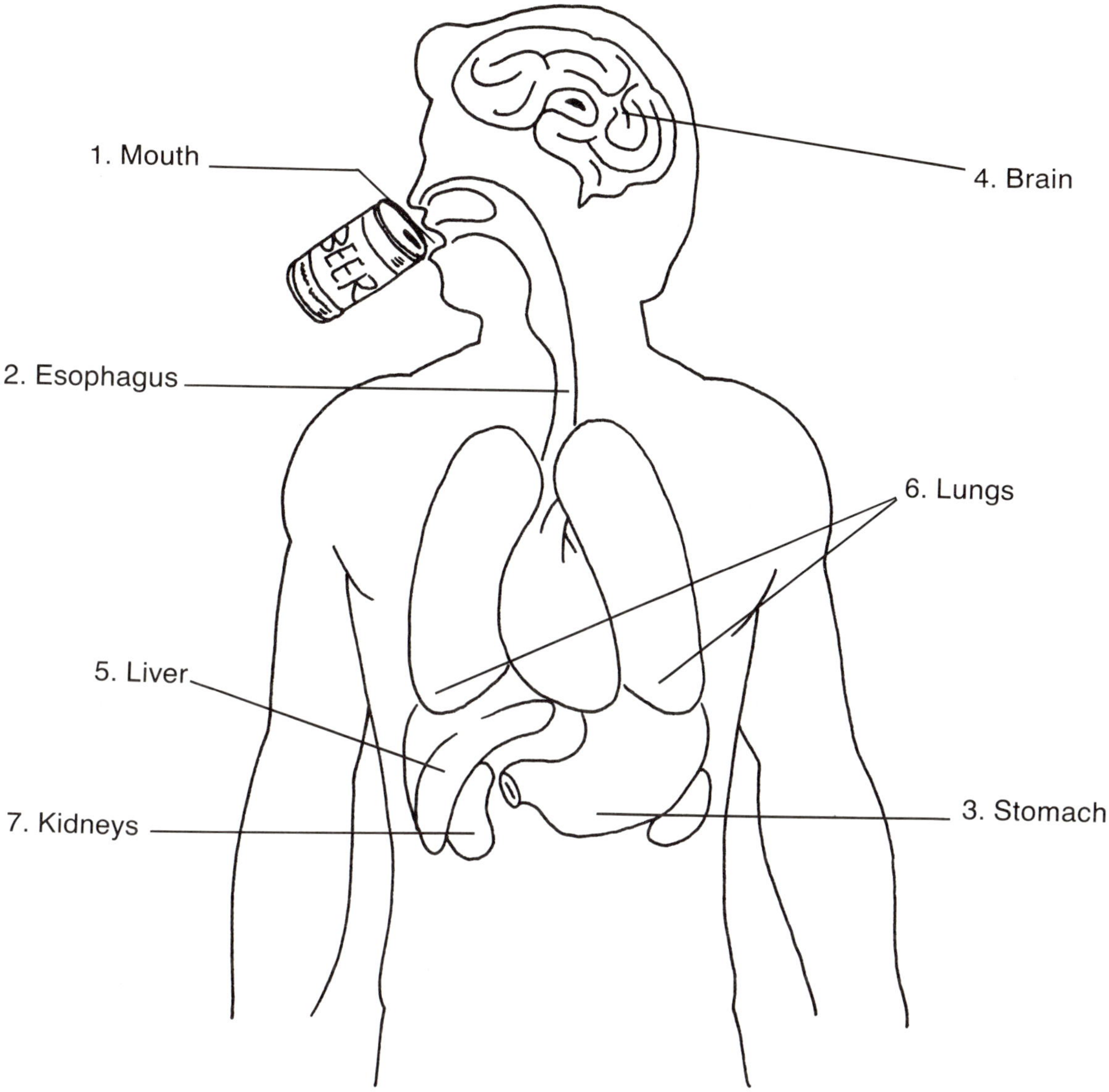

The Path Alcohol Takes Through Your Body

1. You drink alcohol through your **mouth.**
2. The drink makes its way down the **esophagus.**
3. About twenty percent of the alcohol is absorbed into the bloodstream through the **stomach.**
4. The bloodstream carries it to the **brain** as well as the rest of the body.
5. The other eighty percent of the alcohol not absorbed through the stomach goes to the **liver,** where most of it is broken down into carbon dioxide and water.
6. The carbon dioxide is passed out of the **lungs.**
7. The water is passed out of the body via the **kidneys.**

How Alcohol Acts on the Body

When a person drinks one dose of alcohol (see "Defining a Drink," page 47), it takes about fifteen minutes for it to get to the bloodstream. This means it is carried to all parts of the body quickly—including the brain.

The brain is like the cockpit of a plane. It's the control center for our bodies, and it's very sensitive to alcohol. Doctors think alcohol depresses (stops or slows) a part of the brain that controls different parts of the body. We don't think much about being able to stand, walk, and speak with ease, but these are complex actions that are all coordinated by the central nervous system, located in the brain and spine. As the level of alcohol rises in the body, the nervous system works less and less efficiently.

After the first drink or two, (around 0.05 blood alcohol level) a drinker may only show a change in alertness, perhaps by not paying as much attention to what people around him are saying. As he has a little more, the drinker loses fine movement control—he'll spill his drink when he's trying to pour more or bump into furniture. Because drinking affects inhibitions (self-control), he might talk more or louder than usual, flirt with women he wouldn't normally flirt with, dance when he's never danced before.

When the drinker's blood alcohol content reaches a higher point (between 0.10 and 0.15), he will walk or stand unsteadily. His lack of fine movement control is even more pronounced; writing a letter, driving a car, washing dishes, having sex, or anything else involving his muscles might be hopeless. Other abilities are reduced, too: Although he can hear sounds, he might have trouble distinguishing between them and judging their direction. When he hears his wife calling, he thinks it's coming from the downstairs kitchen instead of the upstairs bedroom. Alcohol also affects the drinker's sense of time and space (five hours in a bar might seem like fifteen minutes); his vision (if he's driving, a red light won't look as red as it should); his smell and taste (he could eat a whole dinner without really paying attention to it); his emotions (he might start fights, cry over silly things, dare to do something risky, act very sexy—in other words, act on impulse or feelings rather than on thought or judgment).

As the blood alcohol content gets dangerously higher, the drinker is barely able to speak clearly or walk without staggering. His perception of pain is awry, too; if he went out in the freezing cold, he probably wouldn't feel it. He could fall and hurt himself, but he might not realize it.

At the highest stage of intoxication, a drinker becomes unconscious. When the blood alcohol percentage is more than 0.35, death is possible.

Q. What is a "blood alcohol level"?

A. The percentage of alcohol in a person's blood is the measure that highway patrol officers use to determine if a driver is drunk. A blood alcohol level of ten percent or 0.10 means one part alcohol to 1,000 parts blood, which in most states is legally drunk, leads to a charge of "Driving While Intoxicated" (DWI). Even at 0.05, a drinker's driving skills aren't up to par, which has resulted in some states lowering their DWI requirement to this level. The laws vary, so make sure you know yours. At the same time, remember that individuals react differently to alcohol. A blood alcohol content of 0.03 isn't comfortable for everyone. It's best not to drink and drive at all. (See "Social Problems," page 64.)

Even if you don't drink—or drive—you can be seriously affected by someone who does. Drunk drivers are as dangerous to their passengers and other people on the road as they are to themselves.

Q. *How many drinks does it take for a person to be "legally drunk"?*

A. It depends on the person and the conditions.

1. First, a large person takes longer to get drunk than someone who is smaller. For example, a 100-pound person who has between three and four drinks in two hours probably has a blood alcohol level of 0.10. (See "Defining a Drink," page 47.) But a 150-pound person will be at 0.10 after five drinks in two hours. Women tend to get intoxicated quicker, too. Why? Females have a larger amount of fat in their bodies, which has an effect on alcohol concentration.

2. The faster a person drinks, the less it takes to get drunk. This is because the body takes a while to metabolize each dose of alcohol, so if a person drinks just a little bit more than she can metabolize, her blood alcohol level will increase and she'll become more and more drunk. But if an individual drinks slightly less alcohol each hour than the amount he or she can metabolize, the blood alcohol content remains low.

3. Food in the stomach slows down the rate at which alcohol is absorbed in the bloodstream because it "coats" the stomach first, then dilutes (waters down) the alcohol. So alcohol is likely to "zap" a meal-skipper faster than the drinker with a full stomach.

4. A person's mood makes a difference, too. If an individual drinks when he's sad, alcohol will probably depress him more. If that same person drinks at a wedding, he's likely to feel happy, even though alcohol is a depressant.

6. Setting also influences a drinker. A woman who's having a drink or two with her boss will probably be less effected than when she's with her friends at a bar.

7. Finally, the drink itself: Straight shots of liquor, which are more concentrated doses of alcohol, are absorbed faster than alcohol mixed with milk or water, or beer and wine, which have ingredients other than alcohol. However, alcohol mixed with soda is quickly absorbed, since the carbonation makes it easier for alcohol to get into the bloodstream.

How Drinking Alcohol Makes You Feel

Eileen is just sipping her second drink, and already she is feeling a little "happier." When she first got to the party, she was uptight, but this drink is helping her to relax, loosen up, and forget her problems at work. She feels this way because alcohol is a depressant; at first, it makes you feel "up," but when alcohol goes to work on your brain, it actually takes you down—hence, Eileen's relaxation.

As Eileen finishes her second drink and starts her third, she feels warm, her face flushed. Alcohol causes blood vessels near the skin to dilate (get larger). As the alcohol has more effect on her brain, she feels more emotional than usual. Her friend, Leslie, is at the party, and she feels closer than ever to her.

In fact, when she starts her fourth drink, she tells Leslie this several times and confesses things about her husband that she would never tell if she weren't drinking. It doesn't bother Eileen now; she thinks she feels great, but she isn't consciously thinking now. She's not thinking about how much she's drinking or how she's laughing louder than usual. Nor does she notice that she's spilling her drink on her dress. As she gets up to go to the restroom time after time (because alcohol stimulates hormones that affect the kidneys, causing frequent urination), she gets a little clumsier.

Yet, Eileen is still feeling good in a fuzzy sort of way. Because she's drinking alcohol faster than her body can metabolize, her judgment, alertness, coordination, and other everyday control skills are being depressed by alcohol.

Luckily, by the time Eileen has her fifth drink, she *does* realize she's drunk. She's beginning to feel tired and sleepy, and she can't walk without wobbling or talk without slurring her words. Try as she might, she can't cover it up, either: She can't get total control of herself. It's also lucky that even when she's intoxicated, she knows *not* to get behind the wheel. She lets her friends drive her home. But who knows? If she had been a little drunker, perhaps her judgment would have been so "shot" that she wouldn't have realized what a mistake driving would be.

When Eileen falls into bed, she feels slightly dizzy, almost as if the room really was spinning around her. The spinning room makes her *nauseous*, so she feels sick and vomits. Eventually, she falls into a hard sleep.

Is it like this for everyone? Not always. Eileen is only one person. Some people react to alcohol by getting depressed and crying easily, instead of getting happy like Eileen. Others get sleepy earlier than Eileen, but some can continue to drink for quite a while without feeling sleepy. A few drinkers get mean; they want to yell, argue, or fight. Still other people feel like getting romantic or taking risks, such as trying to swim across a lake in the dark. Unlike Eileen, some people don't get sick, but many do. (See "Next-Day Blues," page 56.)

Even though one woman can react to alcohol in different ways from day to day (depending on the person and the conditions), Eileen's experience gives you an idea of what it's like. Alcohol makes almost everyone feel relaxed and comfortable at first. As more alcohol is consumed, it continues to make you feel good, but it's more like a dream world. Nothing around you is clear—not for your eyes, ears, or head—and you're not in control of yourself anymore. Alcohol is. Only time will get you back in control.

Slowing Down Alcohol

To slow down the effects of alcohol, a person should:
(A) Snack while drinking;
(B) Eat something before beginning to drink;
(C) Drink more slowly.

© Terry Qing/FPG International

Substance abuse causes pain and unhappiness. Frequent episodes of intoxication result in underachievement in school, the loss of good friends who become intolerant of the problem drinker's actions, and sometimes physical harm or legal problems.

Why Teens Say They Drink

Reasons Teens Give for Drinking Alcohol

- Because they're curious about it
- Because they're celebrating something
- Because their friends do
- Because their parents do
- Because they want to relax
- Because it feels good
- Because they want to look older or more sophisticated
- Because they want to break rules
- Because they want to get away from problems

Reasons Teens Give for Not Drinking

- Because it's against the law for young people
- Because they don't want to look silly or lose control
- Because their parents would be upset
- Because their friends would disapprove
- Because they don't want a hangover
- Because they are concerned about health
- Because they don't want the extra calories
- Because they want to concentrate on important things
- Because they don't need it to have a good time

Q. *Does alcohol have any nutritional value?*

A. Alcohol supplies plenty of calories but no nutrients. A five-ounce glass of wine has about 114 calories; a bottle of regular beer about 148. "Light" beers don't save many calories, either; even if they manage to get down to ninety calories, that's ninety "empty calories." Theoretically, you can drink a whole meal of calories with six drinks or so, without getting a thing to nourish your body. In fact, drinkers sometimes suffer from vitamin deficiencies because they tend to skip meals and snack on foods like pretzels and peanuts. What's more, alcohol depletes the body's supply of some specific vitamins and water. (See "Nutrition.")

Next-Day Blues

Eileen only felt a little dizzy when she went to bed, but when she woke up, she felt a lot more.

For one thing, alcohol changes sleep patterns. It sure put Eileen to sleep in a hurry, but Eileen woke up much earlier than she normally would. Although she was still very tired when she woke up, she had trouble getting back to sleep, since alcohol interfered with the usual light-to-deep sleep pattern that she normally experiences.

Why didn't she just get up? Because she had a hangover—a condition that makes you feel like doing nothing. The more a person drinks and the faster she drinks, the greater the chance of a hangover. Eileen's liver didn't have time to break down all the alcohol she consumed, and it accumulated in her bloodstream. The results: a throbbing headache, caused by an enlargement of the head's blood vessels; nausea, because alcohol irritates the stomach's lining; thirst, due to frequent urination the night before; dizziness, resulting from an alcohol-induced drop in blood sugar. Plus, Eileen feels unusually tired, for many reasons: her sleep patterns were disrupted; she's sick; and she was so intoxicated last night, she didn't realize that she overexerted herself.

TF True or False?

You can cure a hangover with black coffee and a cold shower.

False. Time is the best cure for a hangover, because the only way for alcohol to get out of the body is through the liver. (Only a very small percentage is passed out of the body by breathing and urinating.)

Have you heard the one about the college freshman who goes to a fraternity party—and dies because he drinks too much beer too fast?

It's sad, but true. These kinds of stories are often in the news. It's easy to take drinking alcohol casually—until someone gets hurt. Drinking large amounts of alcohol at one time may lead to paralysis of one nerve center in the brain after another. Finally, the nerve centers that control the heart and lungs may become paralyzed. The result is death from alcohol poisoning.

People don't die or get brain damage just at college parties. Anytime a person overdoes alcohol—at home, at a dance, on a camping trip—he's taking a big risk, not only because his system could suffer, but also because he's more prone to accidents. One-third to one-half of all fatal accidents (*other* than traffic accidents) are associated with alcohol use.

Facts About Teens and Alcohol

Compared to nondrinking teens, studies show that young people who drink alcohol have a greater chance of:

- Not learning the things necessary for a healthy and safe life.
- Getting involved with other drugs, such as cigarettes and marijuana.
- Getting in trouble with the law.
- Having a drinking problem later in life.
- Getting in trouble with parents, friends, and teachers.

© Donato Leo/FPG International

ALCOHOL

	NEGATIVE	POSITIVE
SHORT-TERM CONSEQUENCES	• Interferes with normal functioning: sight, taste, hearing, smell, speech, coordination, concentration • Interrupts sleep patterns • Indigestion, loss of appetite • Hangovers • Accident risks • Crime risks • Loss of control around others • Expense	• Euphoria (intense happiness) • Relaxation • Confidence • Makes you feel older, sophisticated • Helps you feel "accepted" • Helps you forget problems, temporarily
LONG-TERM CONSEQUENCES	• Damage to the liver, pancreas, stomach, muscles, heart, and other organs • Damage to the brain: memory defects, psychiatric problems • Vitamin deficiencies • Abnormal pregnancies • Reduced immunity to disease • Impotence in males • Withdrawal symptoms • Alcoholism • Others see you as socially unskilled, inept	

Short-Term Gains vs. Long-Term Losses

Alcohol abuse, as you can see, is a lot like tobacco abuse. The immediate consequences may seem positive—although a hangover is no bowl of cherries. On the negative side, even the experienced drinker can make an intoxicated mistake, such as driving or falling and injuring himself.

Still, many drinkers will put up with an occasional drunk night and an early morning headache because they enjoy the short-term relaxation and euphoria. Yet when alcohol is abused, the health risks are anything but happy.

Don't Drink While Baby's on the Way

If your mother became pregnant, one of the first things her doctor would tell her is "don't drink." When pregnant women drink alcohol, it gets to the unborn baby via the bloodstream. Women who take three drinks a day, three or more times a week, may deliver a baby with fetal alcohol syndrome. When this happens, the infant has some or several of these disorders: abnormally low weight; heart defects; abnormal facial features, such as small, wide-set eyes; mental retardation; sleep disorders. Often, the baby doesn't grow up to be normal, physically or mentally.

Not that a mother has to be a chronic drinker to have pregnancy problems. Even moderate drinkers can deliver an under-weight baby. Low levels of alcohol increase the risk of miscarriage and other problems, too. So the best rule for pregnant women is: not a drop. (See "Human Sexuality.")

***Alcohol:** a clear, colorless liquid that is made by brewing sugar with yeast. Examples: whiskey, beer, wine, vodka.*

Physical Problems: Alcohol is a chemical, so it makes sense that when a person drinks too much for too long, the body can get damaged.

Even after a few weeks of four or five drinks a day, the liver begins to show the first signs of health problems. (Remember that almost all alcohol has to be metabolized by the liver, so this organ takes the brunt of the abuse.) Prolonged drinking scars the liver, so that the disease cirrhosis may develop. In its early stages, cirrhosis causes few symptoms, but in advanced stages, the liver fails to do its work, possibly resulting in coma or death. Ten to fifteen percent of all alcoholics suffer from cirrhosis, the sixth leading cause of death in the United States. In addition, other disorders of the liver are common health problems for chronic drinkers.

Vitamin Deficiencies: These may be responsible for various diseases afflicting the brain, the digestive tract, the muscles, and the heart. Many heavy drinkers neglect their diets because alcohol contains a lot of calories but no nutrients. It's also possible that alcohol affects the body's absorption of vitamins—especially thiamine—in some way. (See "Nutrition.")

Brain Damage: Another alcohol-related health problem, brain damage is second only to Alzheimer's disease as a cause of mental deterioration, when people gradually lose their memories and other mental abilities. Very heavy drinkers may also experience emotional problems as a result of their brain damage: Paranoia (feeling like people are "out to get you"), jealousy, and delusions (not seeing situations as they really are) can become real psychiatric disorders. Two out of every five males admitted to state mental hospitals suffer from alcoholism.

Heart Problems: Although it's not clear that the relationship is direct, excessive drinking has been linked to heart trouble. For one thing, alcoholics frequently are heavy smokers, so doctors aren't always sure if smoking or drinking is responsible for ill health. It could also be that a drinker's poor diet—and not his drinking—causes heart disease.

Other Problems: Alcohol is carried by the bloodstream to all parts of the body (see "The Path Alcohol Takes Through Your Body," page 49), making alcoholics vulnerable to various inflammations of the stomach, intestines, kidneys, and lungs. Other diseases—asthma, gout, diabetes—are also more common among alcoholics. Doctors also suspect a cancer connection, but once again, it's hard to tell the cigarette problems from the alcohol problems. Though all the research isn't in on how alcohol damages the body, suffice it to say that alcohol abusers shorten their life spans by ten to twelve years.

Q. What are withdrawal symptoms?

A. One night of heavy drinking results in a hangover. Several days, weeks, or months of drinking will trigger a much more serious physical reaction: withdrawal symptoms.

Just as the body becomes dependent on cigarettes or drugs, it gets used to alcohol. When the supply is stopped or drastically cut down, the drinker may experience the "jitters" or shakes; nausea and vomiting; weakness or an achy feeling; depression; dry mouth; restless sleep; and so on. In a few extreme cases, seizures or delirium tremens (a state characterized by wild dreams, confusion, being "out if it") may occur.

Withdrawal symptoms usually begin right after a heavy drinker changes his drinking habits and almost always disappear within five to seven days.

Some teens show a dramatic behavioral change when they're intoxicated; they may become loud and offensive, rebellious and mean, sexually aggressive, or boring.

Defining an Alcoholic and Alcohol Abuse

There are all kinds of definitions and opinions about what makes an alcoholic an alcoholic, as well as what constitutes alcohol abuse. We won't go into all the different distinctions here, but for your purposes, here are signs that alcohol is a big problem:

- Doing things while drinking that are regretted later
- Drinking alone or "on the sly"
- Depending on alcohol to get through difficult situations
- Drinking every day
- Drinking in the morning or at other unusual times
- Changing types of alcohol in order to control drinking
- Having problems at home, work, or school because of drinking
- Feeling uncomfortable when alcohol is not available
- "Passing out" while drinking
- Drinking in risky situations, like before driving

As you can see, a person doesn't really have to be physically dependent or even a so-called "heavy drinker" to abuse alcohol. Nor does a person have to experience *all* the criteria above to have an alcohol problem; just one will do it. Any time a person is not always in control of when he begins or ends drinking, he's abusing alcohol. (If you know anyone who fits any of these descriptions, see Part II.)

TF True or False?

Alcoholics are rarely the stereotypical skid-row bum.

True. The pathetic down-and-outers you see sleeping in doorways account for only a small percentage of the total alcoholic population—probably less than five percent. The other ninety percent are college professors, physicians, construction workers, lawyers, priests—people who are all around us. Perhaps they don't pop open a can of beer at ten o'clock in the morning or drink a quart of scotch a day, but they're drinking irresponsibly in other ways.

Social Problems: The physical health risks that drinkers take are threatening, but at least an individual is in control of decreasing—or increasing—his own risk. When it comes to social problems, however, *other* people are victimized by someone else's alcohol abuse.

Drunk Driving: Not only are problem drinkers risking their own death or injury in accidents, they put other people in danger. One of the nation's biggest social problems is drunk driving. Unfortunately, many drivers think alcohol improves instead of impairs their driving. Yet, studies show that drinking even a little increases a person's chances of having an automobile accident. (See What is a "blood alcohol level"? page 51.)

The statistics prove it, too: Every twenty-one minutes, someone in the United States is killed by a drunk driver, a total of seventy men, women, and children every day. On the average, one out of every ten drivers on the road is drunk. More bad news: Young people are disproportionately represented among these risk takers. In 1983, sixteen-to-twenty-four-year-olds made up only twenty percent of the nation's population, but they constituted thirty-four percent of the drivers killed in alcohol-related accidents. According to a 1985 report by the New York State Division of Alcoholism and Alcohol Abuse, drivers twenty years and younger represented only seven percent of all licensed drivers; but that seven percent was responsible for twenty-one percent of the drivers in fatal alcohol-related crashes.

Crime Rate: One-third to one-half of all crimes committed are associated with alcohol use. This includes homicide (the killing of one person by another), sexual abuse, spouse abuse, child abuse, assault (a violent physical or verbal attack), robbery, and so on. Authorities believe that alcohol abuse among young people is an important contributing factor to juvenile delinquency (a law violation by a person under eighteen).

Home Life: According to the National Institute on Alcohol Abuse and Alcoholism, at least four other persons are affected by an alcoholic's behavior. If there are about ten million problem drinkers and alcoholics in the country, that means forty million people share alcohol problems second-hand. The problem is so common that several organizations have been set up to help the families and friends of chronic drinkers. (See "Where to Get Help," page 112.)

Perhaps most affected of all are the children of alcoholics. In general, life with an alcoholic parent can be characterized by fear (worry that an intoxicated parent will hurt or embarrass them), tension (unrest among the family members, e.g., "will Mom be drunk again tonight?"), inconsistency (one day Dad is like "old times," the next day he's drunk again), conflict (fights, arguments, scolding), and blame (parents tell their kids they drink because the kids are being "bad," and make the kids feel guilty). Perhaps troubled home lives are partially responsible for the fact that children of alcoholics are more likely to be alcoholics than children of nonalcoholics. (See "Growing Up with Alcohol," page 67.)

DRINKING ON THE ROAD

If your blood alcohol content is:	Your risk of being involved in a traffic accident is:
0.10 percent	7 times out of 100 **7%**
0.15 percent	1 time out of 14 **25%**
0.18 percent	3 times out of 5 **60%**
0.20 percent	10 times out of 10 **100%**

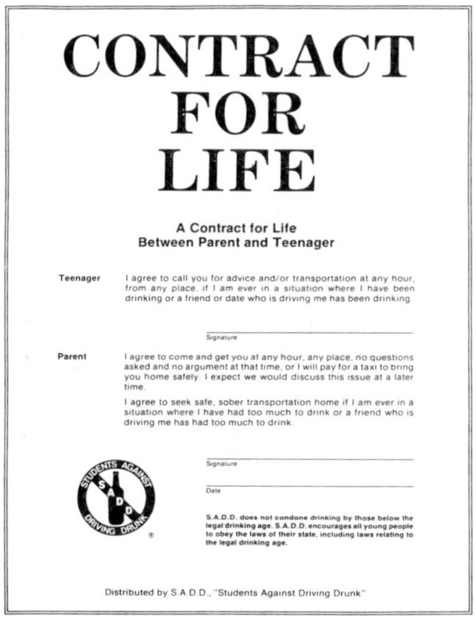

CONTRACT FOR LIFE

A Contract for Life
Between Parent and Teenager

Teenager I agree to call you for advice and/or transportation at any hour, from any place, if I am ever in a situation where I have been drinking or a friend or date who is driving me has been drinking.

Signature

Parent I agree to come and get you at any hour, any place, no questions asked and no argument at that time, or I will pay for a taxi to bring you home safely. I expect we would discuss this issue at a later time.

I agree to seek safe, sober transportation home if I am ever in a situation where I have had too much to drink or a friend who is driving me has had too much to drink.

Signature

Date

STUDENTS AGAINST DRIVING DRUNK S A D D

S.A.D.D. does not condone drinking by those below the legal drinking age. S.A.D.D. encourages all young people to obey the laws of their state, including laws relating to the legal drinking age.

Distributed by S.A.D.D., "Students Against Driving Drunk"

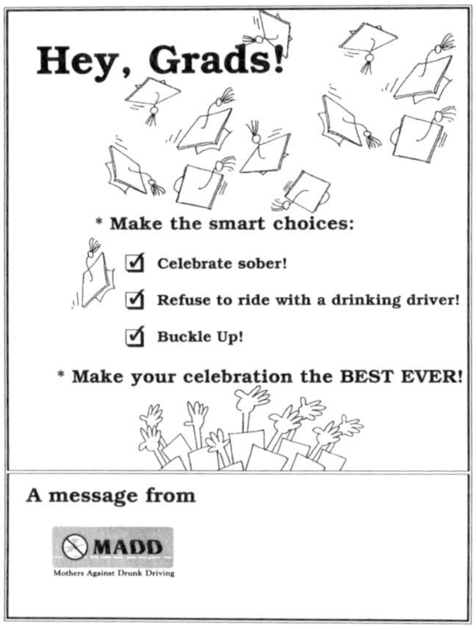

Mothers Against Drunk Drivers (M.A.D.D.) and Students Against Drunk Driving (S.A.D.D.) are two organizations that were formed to educate people about the dangers of driving drunk. (For more on M.A.D.D. and S.A.D.D., see page 103.)

Q. *What do teens really think about drinking and driving?*

A. According to recent research by the NIAA, one in three teens thinks some people can drive safely after drinking. Another surprising figure: four in ten teens between thirteen and fifteen have at some time been a passenger in a car driven by someone about their own age who was under the influence of alcohol or drugs. Scary! For more information, see ''Passing Up the Passenger Seat,'' page 102.

Growing Up with Alcohol

A relatively new organization called ACOA (Adult Children of Alcoholics) says that more than twenty-two million adults in the United States grew up with an alcoholic in the house. This group is concerned because their members still have problems in their day-to-day lives, yet they're not children anymore and they don't have to live with an alcoholic parent. A few of the traits they share:

- They don't know how to have fun.
- They're either extremely responsible or irresponsible.
- They have difficulty in completing projects.
- They lie when it's easy to tell the truth.
- They judge themselves strictly and often have low self-esteem.
- They find it difficult to get emotionally close to people.
- They're afraid of change.

Not all children of alcoholics have these problems, but there is help for people who do. If one of your parents is an alcoholic or has a drinking problem, see page 112.

Alcoholism: A Family Affair?

Why is it that sons of alcoholics are twice as likely as others to become alcoholics themselves? Some scientists recently set out to find the answer. Their results aren't final, but it's quite likely they're true.

For one thing, there is evidence that suggests the predisposition to alcohol is genetic rather than learned behavior. In other words, the son of the alcoholic doesn't necessarily *learn* to become alcoholic; he inherits it, just as he inherits his dad's brown eyes or height. There isn't an alcoholic gene, but there is something about a person's physiology—the way he metabolizes alcohol or how rapidly it affects him, for example—that can increase the chance that alcohol will become a problem.

The doctors found that babies of an alcoholic father who were adopted by nonalcoholic parents were four times more likely to have drinking problems by the time the boys reached their early twenties than adopted children whose biological parents were nondrinkers. Researchers suspect that some people are more affected by alcohol than others and this judgment problem can be passed on.

This concept carried even more clout when researchers found that if one identical twin had a drinking problem, the other one was more likely to have one, too. The same hasn't proved true for fraternal twins, however. (Females haven't been as well-studied as males, since only recently have statistics shown alcohol to be a major problem for them, too.)

The last thing you want to do is take this study as gospel and *expect* the child of a heavy drinker to do the same. But it helps to know if you are among this high-risk group. If alcoholism is part of your family history, you can take steps now to avoid your personal abuse. See Part II.

The Business Side of Alcohol

In spite of alarming statistics that peg tobacco products as a major health hazard, their manufacturers still play an important role in the nation's economy. The money they put into taxes and advertising influences different groups—including the United States government—to "smooth over" the problems smoking causes.

Alcohol isn't quite as dangerous; some adults can have an occasional drink without letting it ruin their health (unlike cigarettes—even one is bad news). Yet, alcohol advertisers also distort the image of drinking, causing it to be even more of a problem.

Think of the beer commercials you see on television. The guys are in bars, having a great time, telling funny jokes. That may be true-to-life, but beer advertisers don't show you what sometimes happens *after* the party. Somebody gets in the car, thinking he can drive as well as usual, and might get arrested for DWI, get hurt in an accident, or kill himself and others. Wine cooler advertisers play great music and show sand, surf, and bikinis, but they don't show you alcoholics who are dying of liver disease. Then there are liquor advertisements that don't really have anything to do with drinking; like cigarette ads, they just show you an attractive couple or a beautiful mountain stream to get you to associate good things with alcohol.

It's true alcohol manufacturers don't show teenagers getting drunk, and some do sponsor campaigns against drunk driving and heavy drinking. Yet, it's important to see these ads for what they are: an attempt to get you to buy a product so manufacturers can make more money. They don't care if you have a good time or not.

Here's another practical point to consider: The money spent on treatment for alcoholism and alcoholic-related diseases in this country is unbelievable (about $14.9 billion in 1983). A lot of money is also spent on crime, welfare, employee replacement, and other losses associated with alcohol.

TF

True or False?

As drinking increases, so does other addictive behavior.

True. You already know that people who take one kind of risk are more apt to take another kind. Alcohol drinkers are a specific example. A 1985 report by the New York State Division of Alcoholism and Alcohol Abuse stated: "Alcohol [is] the drug of choice among the young and is the most widely misused drug. Marijuana is commonly used with alcohol, increasing the risks to this population." A survey from the February 1987 issue of *Ms.* magazine reported the same correlation: "As drinking increases, moreover, so does other addictive behavior. It was . . . clear that the more women drank, the more likely they were to smoke cigarettes, marijuana, and hashish."

Drugs: Disease That Won't Leave

Nonprescription, mood-altering drugs don't have the history that cigarettes and alcohol have. In fact, the National Institute on Drug Abuse has said that before 1960 drug abuse by young people was generally unheard of. Although small groups of people had problems with heroin after World War II in the 1940s and the Korean War in the 1950s, it didn't last long; not only did the supplies left over from the wars run out, citizens generally did not approve of drug abuse.

Things changed quickly in the 1960s and 1970s. For many reasons related to social changes, young people turned to different substances. In 1962, only one percent of twelve-to-seventeen-year-olds had ever used marijuana, but in 1972, almost one-third had. In 1984, about one-fourth of high-school seniors reported using marijuana.

These days, health experts are less concerned about teens' use of drugs such as heroin and LSD. Although these drugs were very popular in the 1960s and early 1970s, the numbers have fallen in the 1980s. The problem drugs for young people today seem to be marijuana, amphetamines, and forms of cocaine.

During the Vietnam War, many American soldiers got into the habit of using heroin, pictured here. They used it to make the time pass more quickly, they said. Experts predicted that the soldiers would become addicted, but in fact, most of them stopped using heroin when they got home. The point is that sometimes the environment you live in can cause you to make the mistake of trying drugs, but there is always a chance that you'll become addicted.

© AGE Fotostock/FPG International

Defining Drugs and Drug Abuse

When your doctor writes you a prescription, or when you go to the drug store for cough medicine, you're getting drugs that are controlled and intended to restore or maintain health. Doctors' prescriptions have more potential to be harmful if used incorrectly, but that's why doctors tell you exactly *how* to use them. Over-the-counter drugs don't need a doctor's approval because they are thought to be safe enough for the average consumer to take without a doctor's guidance. Government agencies watch all of these products closely. (See "Maintaining Good Health.")

Mood-altering "street drugs" don't fit this description. Although doctors do prescribe some of them for various reasons (painkillers, emotional problems), when people talk about substance abuse, they usually mean "psychoactive drugs," or chemicals taken because they change the way a person thinks or feels. They're also known as street drugs because using them is illegal: they're not prescription and they're being used in ways that are harmful. Street drugs aren't always bought on the street; anytime they are obtained from an unauthorized person—whether it's a teen at a party or a doctor who's illegally supplying a rock star—they fit into this group of unhealthy substances.

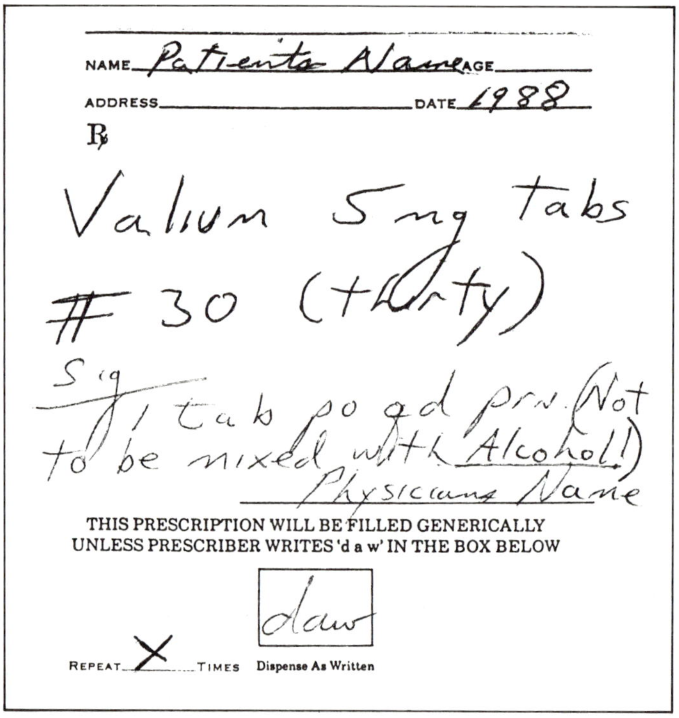
NAME Patients Name AGE
ADDRESS DATE 1988
℞
Valium 5 mg tabs
#30 (thirty)
Sig 1 tab po qd prn. (Not to be mixed with Alcohol!)
Physicians Name
THIS PRESCRIPTION WILL BE FILLED GENERICALLY
UNLESS PRESCRIBER WRITES 'd a w' IN THE BOX BELOW
daw
REPEAT X TIMES Dispense As Written

Drugs and alcohol don't mix. Some drugs, such as Valium, if mixed with alcohol, can cause nausea, vomiting, and even coma and death. Before you take any drug, be sure you know what it can and can't be mixed with while it is in your system.

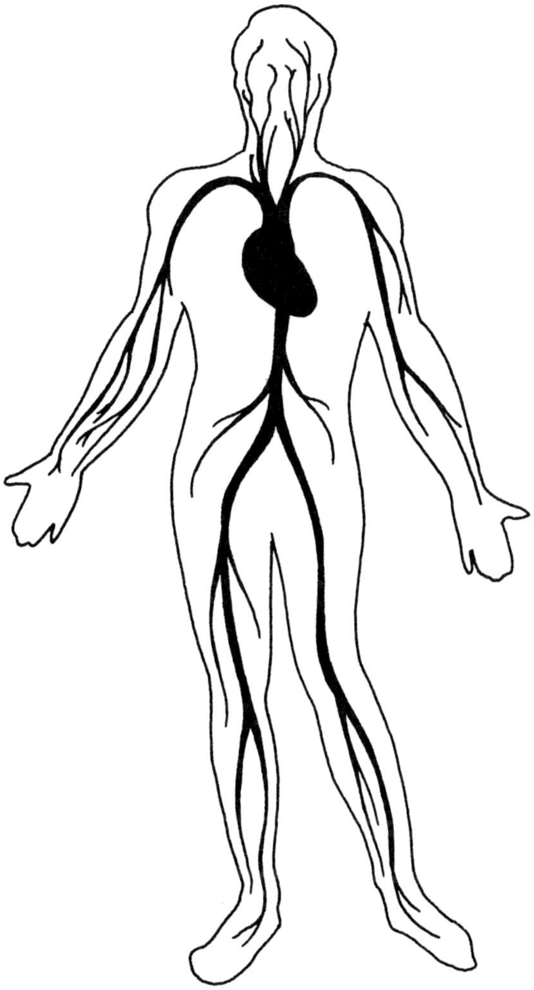

How Drugs Work

Ever since you were a toddler, you've been taking drugs in different ways: you got "shots" before you went to camp; you swallowed aspirin when you had the flu; you inhaled vapors when you had a chest cold. All drugs—illegal or prescription—are administered in one or more of these ways:

Oral dosages: Tablets, capsules, or liquid are taken through the mouth.
Inhalation: Taken into the lungs via the nose and/or mouth.
Subcutaneous injection: A needle syringe pierces and places the drug beneath the skin, usually in the shoulder.
Intramuscular injection: The drug is injected with a syringe into muscle tissue, which has a lot of blood vessels.
Intravenous injection: The drug goes directly from syringe to blood vessel.

Intravenous injections have the fastest results; the drug gets into the bloodstream immediately, then spreads all over the body. Oral dosage is slowest, since the drug is absorbed into the bloodstream from the stomach.

All psychoactive drugs ultimately get into the bloodstream and go to the brain. In fact, the word "psychoactive" means "affecting or changing a person's emotions." These drugs also act on other body parts. For every variety of street drug, there is a description of its effect, both short term and long term.

Teens Talk About Drugs

Reasons Teens Give for Taking Drugs

- Because they're curious
- Because they're bored
- Because it helps them "experience" and see their lives differently
- Because their friends do
- Because drugs help them deal with stress
- Because it makes them feel good
- Because drugs are exciting

Reasons Teens Give for Not Taking Drugs

- Because drugs make them feel good only on a temporary basis
- Because they are dangerous
- Because they are illegal
- Because their families or friends would disapprove
- Because it would hurt their performance at school or in athletics
- Because they don't need them to have a good time
- Because they're afraid of psychoactive drugs

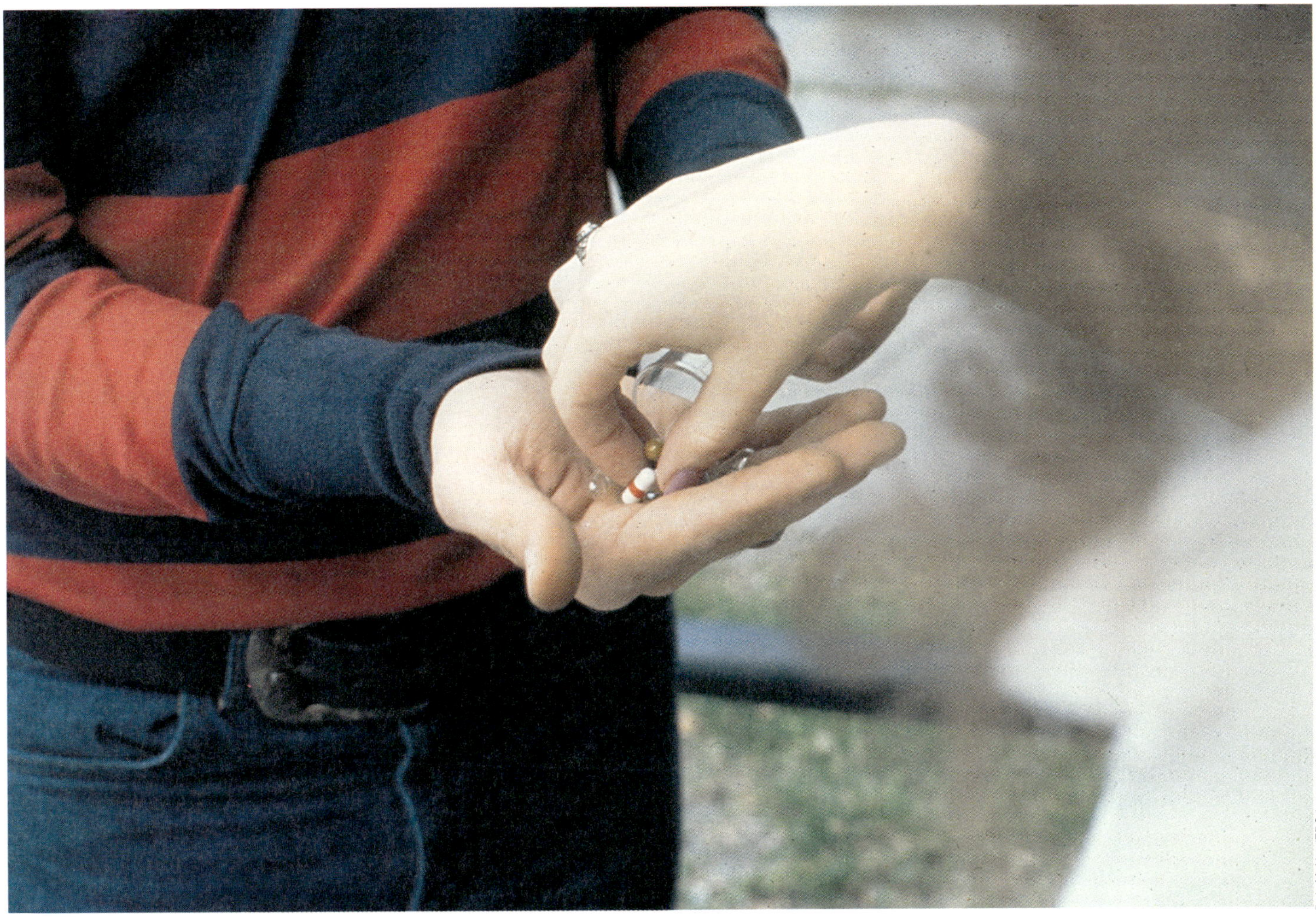

© J. McNee/FPG International

Drugs Can be Divided into Five Major Groups

TYPE OF DRUG	DRUG NAMES	STREET NAMES
DEPRESSANTS	Barbiturates Pentobarbital Secobarbital Amobarbital	Barbs, Downers, Yellow Jackets Red Devils Blue Devils
	Quaalude	Ludes
	Alcohol	Booze, Hooch, Juice, Brew
STIMULANTS	Amphetamines Dextroamphetamine Methamphetamine	Speed, Uppers, Pep Pills, Bennies, Dexies, Moth, Crystal, Black Beauties
	Cocaine	Coke, Snow, Toot, White Lady: Crack
	Nicotine	Coffin, Nail, Butt, Smoke
NARCOTICS	Dilaudid, Percodan, Demerol, Methadone	
	Codeine	School Boy
	Morphine Heroin	Dreamer, Junk, Smack, Horse
HALLUCINOGENS	PCP (Phencyclidine)	Angel Dust, Killer Weed, Supergrass, Hog, Peace Pill
	LSD	Acid, Cubes, Purple Haze
	Mescaline	Mesc, Cactus
	Psilocybin	Magic Mushrooms
MARIJUANA HASHISH		Pot, Grass, Reefer, Weed, Columbian, Hash, Hash Oil, Sinsemilla, Joint

Depressants

Depressants do what their name implies: They slow down the activity of certain areas of the brain and spinal cord. This causes muscles to relax and breathing and heartbeat rates to slow down, too.

Barbiturates are sometimes prescribed by doctors as a sleeping pill, but people use them harmfully when they want a "drunk" feeling.

Short-term effects: Like alcohol, barbiturates can make a person feel good and relaxed at first. Also like alcohol, they slow down reaction time, cause slurred speech and drowsiness, and reduce vision, so driving under their influence is dangerous. Barbiturates can also cause one to have a "hangover" the next day, which could last from hours to days. And if a mother takes barbiturates or other sedatives while she's pregnant, the baby may be born with a physical dependence on the drug or have other serious health problems.

Long-term effects: Addiction and physical dependence develop quickly with these drugs. Going "cold turkey" can be dangerous or even fatal, so medical help—and lots of time—are necessary.

Other dangers: Overdoses can stop a person's breathing by depressing that part of the central nervous system. Combining barbiturates with alcohol is also very risky: The dangers of one multiply the effects of the other. Many accidental deaths have been blamed on a mixture of sleeping pills and alcohol.

TF *True or False?*

Alcohol is a depressant.

True. Alcohol is the most widely used depressant.

© Terry Qing/FPG International

Scientists don't really know why low doses of depressants—such as alcohol and barbiturates—make people feel stimulated. But they do know that, as the dose is increased, parts of the nervous system slow down—and when the high has worn off, the down is* way *down.

Barbiturates are a factor in nearly one-third of all reported drug-related deaths.

It's easy to build up a fast dependence on these drugs (see "How Drug Habits Happen," page 95), so people need more and more of each dose to achieve the "high" they want. This means their judgment and coordination are even more affected than they were with the first doses. Not only are accidents a high-risk possibility, overdoses are, too. Withdrawal symptoms from barbiturates are among the most dangerous of all drug withdrawal symptoms. Some people die because they suddenly stop taking the drug without getting a doctor's help.

Tranquilizers are also prescribed by doctors for people who need medical help, but other people use them illegally for relaxation.

Short-term effects: Some people like tranquilizers because they calm them down without interfering with their alertness and ability to think clearly. They're also long-lasting; because these drugs are absorbed into the bloodstream very slowly, they take longer to reach the brain and could linger from ten hours to days. Like barbiturates, high doses can produce slurred speech, drowsiness, and stupor.

Long-term effects: Painful muscle contractions, slow movement, and permanent problems with coordination are among the dangers from long-term use. Also, using tranquilizers in large doses over long periods of time is addictive. The withdrawal symptoms are very unpleasant (headache, trembling, numbness, nausea) and discontinuing their use has to be done slowly.

Other dangers: Withdrawal or overdose can also result in coma or death.

© G. Marche/FPG International

You can't always tell a book by its cover—or a druggie by the way he or she looks. Today's typical alcoholic or coke fiend isn't a skid-row bum. He or she can be a professional, a student, or a homemaker.

© Christopher Bain

Decaffeinated or caffeine-free soft drinks, teas, and coffees are now widely available, so you can enjoy your favorite drink at any time of the day without caffeine's side effects.

Stimulants

When stimulants are taken, the body processes speed up: The heart beats faster, blood pressure increases, and breathing is faster. The adrenal glands are also stimulated, making the stimulant user feel "up."

Caffeine is the most widely used stimulant in the United States, even more so than nicotine (see "Tobacco," page 20). It's found in coffee, chocolate, tea, cola, and cocoa. It's also used in some over-the-counter drugs, such as diet pills, painkillers, and stay-awake products.

Short-term effects: As the circulatory and respiratory systems speed up, a person feels less tired and more alert. However, if too much caffeine is consumed, insomnia, irritability, headaches, diarrhea, heart palpitations (fast beating), and upset stomach can occur. Other effects include frequent urination and bowel movements and a "letdown" feeling after the stimulant wears off.

Long-term effects: No studies have proven any negative consequences of long-term caffeine use for healthy people. However, caffeine can complicate high blood pressure, peptic ulcers, and premenstrual discomfort. Pregnant women are discouraged from consuming caffeine, too. Some people develop a physical dependence on caffeine, so that if they suddenly stop, they suffer headaches, irritability, and fatigue. (See "Caffeine" above and "Nutrition".)

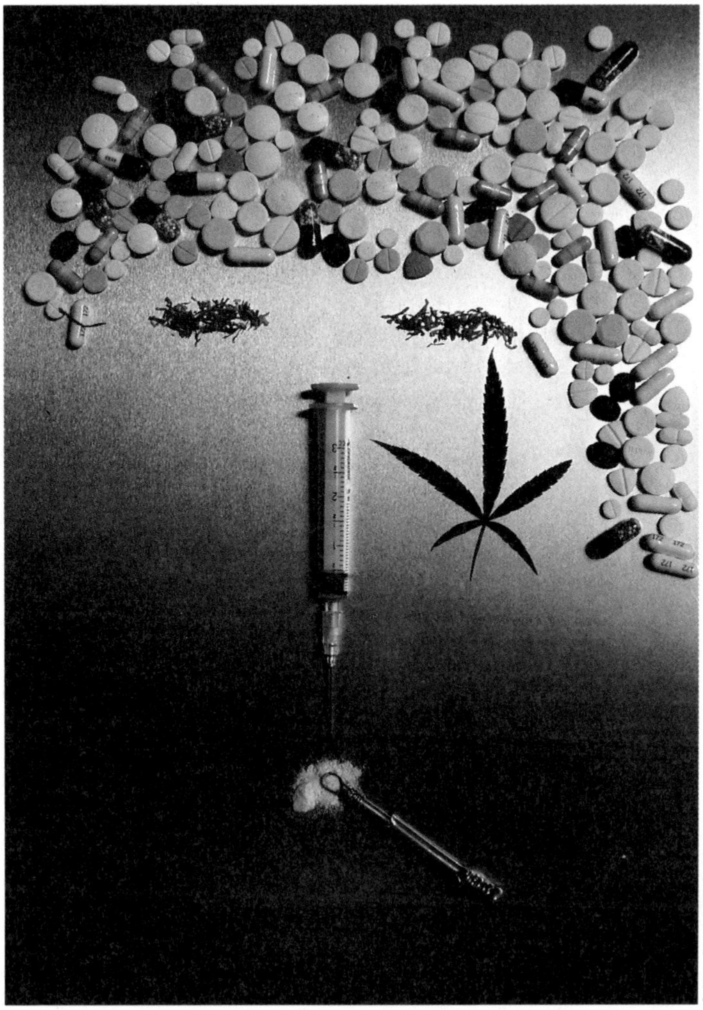

© Elihu Blotnick/FPG International

Amphetamines have been used to treat depression, obesity, sleeping problems, and overactive children. These days, however, doctors believe amphetamines have almost no medical value. When people take amphetamines illegally, it's because they want to stay awake or maintain high energy levels.

Short-term effects: People abuse amphetamines because they produce euphoria and a feeling of well-being, but also because they reduce fatigue and improve concentration and physical performance to a certain extent. However, amphetamine users sometimes experience dry mouth, nervousness, headaches, blurred vision, dizziness, and sweating. Psychologically amphetamine users may be moody, irritable, and at high doses, extremely confident, powerful, and "wired."

Long-term effects: Malnutrition, insomnia, skin disorders, ulcers, depression, and in some cases, brain damage are some of the ill effects from amphetamines. Prolonged use may also result in a psychological disorder, in which the victim sees, hears, and feels things that don't exist; experiences paranoia; or has delusions. Users have been known to develop physical dependence on the drug, which in high doses can lead to a sudden increase in blood pressure, and eventually death from stroke, high fever, or heart failure. Withdrawal symptoms include a very deep sleep that could last for days, intense hunger, depression, and fatigue.

Other dangers: Extremely high doses can also cause irregular or rapid heartbeat, tremors, loss of coordination, and even collapse.

Caffeine Count

How much caffeine do you usually consume in a day? On your own paper, add up a total for the last four days using the chart below as a guide.

Coffee (regular brewed or instant), 1 cup	125 mg
Coffee (freeze-dried instant), 1 cup	70 mg
Coffee (decaffeinated), 1 cup	5 mg
Tea, 1 cup	50 mg
Cocoa, 1 cup	50 mg
Soft drink, 12 ounces	50 mg
Chocolate bar	25 mg

How much did you total for each day? A count of 250 milligrams or more could cause you to experience restlessness, excitement, insomnia, excessive perspiration, heartbeat irregularities, flushed face, muscle twitching, excessive pacing or nervous habits, upset stomach, or diarrhea. Do you have any of these problems? If so, you might cut back on your caffeine intake.

TF True or False?

A good way to "undo" a depressant is to take a stimulant.

False! A stimulant may make you feel "up" for a little while, but when it wears off it will leave you very depressed. Besides, it's dangerous enough to take one nonmedical drug, without adding to the risk by taking another.

In the 1880s, doctors prescribed cocaine for a variety of medical problems since it could numb tissue and soothe the stomach. But soon they realized that prescribing cocaine was a mistake: many patients suffered ill effects or became dependent on it. In the early 1900s, laws were passed against it's use.

Cocaine can be made in laboratories, but it can also be obtained from leaves of coca shrubs grown in South America. Pure cocaine has been used as a local anesthesia for eye, ear, nose, and throat surgery.

How it's used: 1. Fine white crystals are sniffed through the nose. 2. A vapor form is smoked in a pipe (freebasing). 3. A liquid form can also be injected into the veins.

Short-term effects: Cocaine-users experience a short-term intense euphoric state. They may also feel very confident and energetic. At the same time, cocaine can decrease hunger and make a person feel indifferent to pain. Body temperature and blood pressure are higher than usual, and the pupils dilate. However, the "high" is short-lived, from between five to twenty minutes, depending on the type of cocaine used. This means that some people have to take cocaine more frequently to stay "high."

Long-term effects: Some regular users report problems with sleep, restlessness, irritability, and anxiety. Others become paranoid or hallucinate (see things that don't exist). People who sniff or snort cocaine can irritate and damage the insides of their noses, and because cocaine depresses the appetite, some users become unhealthily thin. Frequent freebasers take other big risks: lung damage, heart attacks, or respiratory failure.

Other dangers: Overdoses produce severe stomach pain, convulsions, circulatory failure, respiratory collapse—leading to death. Withdrawal symptoms include anxiety, shakiness, fatigue, depression, and a desire for more cocaine.

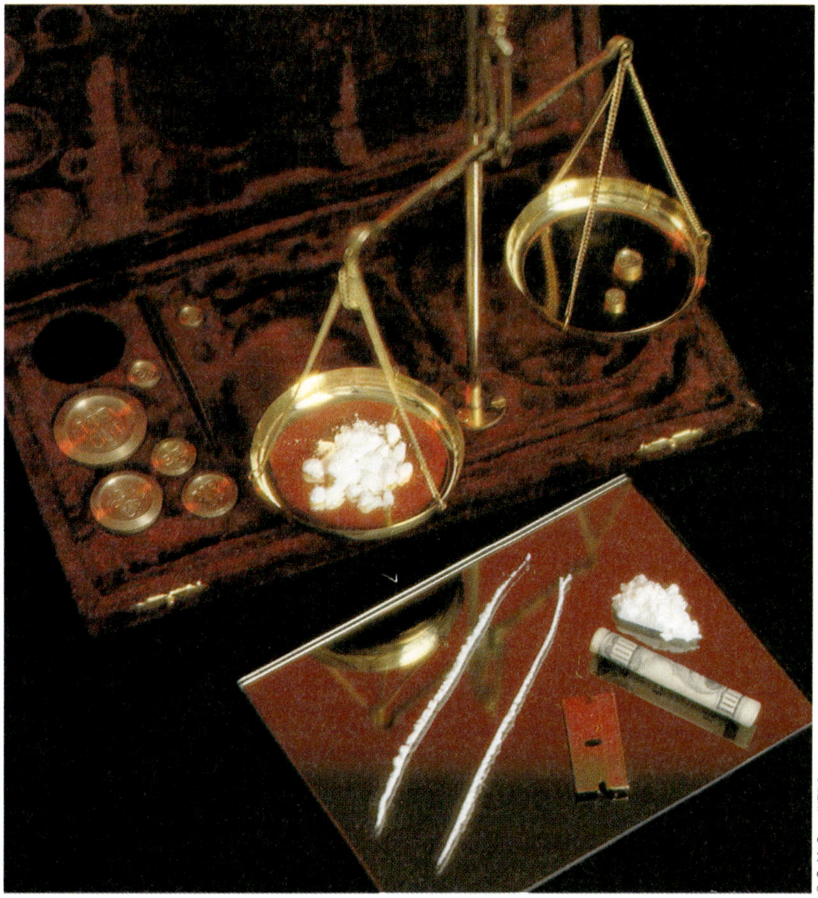

Q. Why is cocaine known as a "glamour" drug?

A. Some forms of cocaine are extremely expensive, costing as much as $2,000 for an ounce. This is why cocaine sold on the streets usually contains large amounts of fillers: powdered sugar, amphetamines, and other substances. Its high price has given cocaine a reputation as the recreational drug for rich people, but in reality, cocaine-abusers are people from all walks of life. This is especially true since alternatives to high-priced cocaine have been found. (See "What's crack?" page 86.)

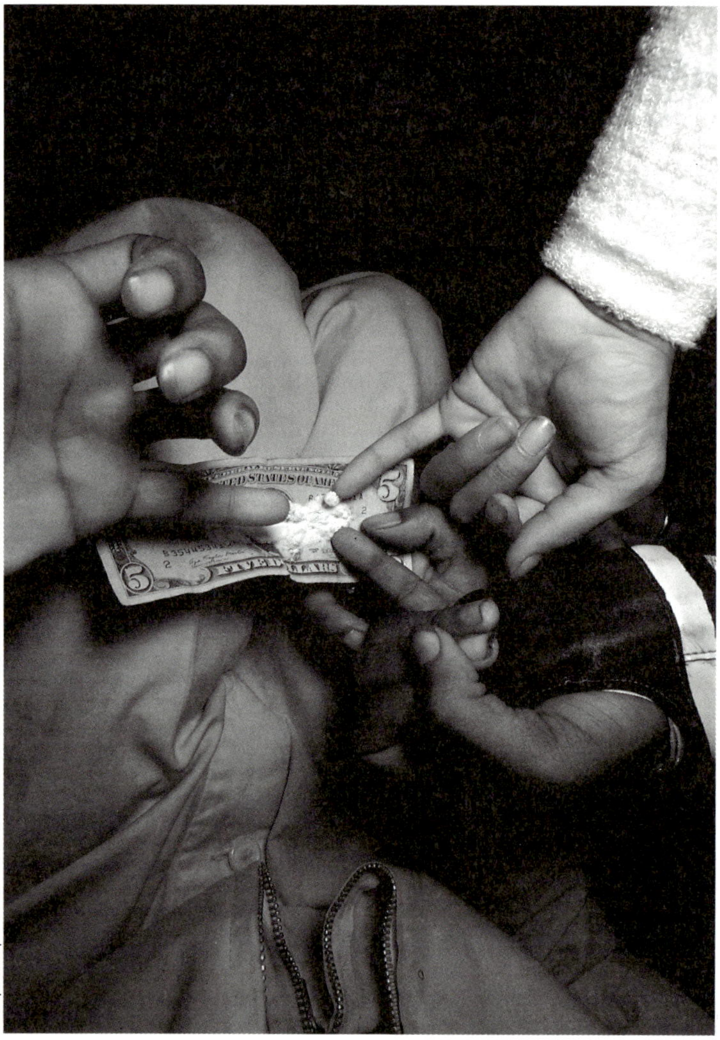

A gram of cocaine, less than a teaspoon, costs at least $100 in many communities. Some users can go through a gram in one night.

Q. *How does cocaine cause death?*

A. Freebasers account for about one third of all cocaine users and are most likely to die as the result of cocaine use. They die not because of overdose, but because the drug is absorbed so quickly: As the blood vessels constrict and the heart muscles rev up, a heart attack or respiratory failure is possible. Freebasing is also dangerous because the method used to turn cocaine into a vapor could cause a fire. Some celebrities' deaths or injuries have been linked to freebase fires.

How Cocaine Harms the Body

Here is a point-by-point breakdown of how cocaine affects the body:

1. The **blood vessels** tighten and **blood pressure** rises quickly.
2. Because the blood vessels tighten, less blood is able to get to the **heart.** This is dangerous because blood carries oxygen to the heart. The lack of sufficient oxygen could cause painful spasms in the heart (angina), irregular or increased heartbeat, or even a heart attack. There is also a chance of permanent, long-term damage to the heart, which, unfortunately, may not be recognized until it's too late.
3. Oxygen to the **brain and nervous system** may also be restricted, putting the body at risk of stroke. Cocaine can also cause seizures or tremors, in the brain and nervous system.
4. Cocaine users have suffered spasms in the **abdomen** due to lack of blood supply.
5. For unexplained reasons, the drug has also triggered an accumulation of fluids in the **lungs.** Cocaine-users have been known to ''drown'' from this condition.
6. Cocaine is either sniffed, injected, or smoked. When it's sniffed, the chemical is so strong that it damages the lining of the **nose.** This leads to holes between the nostrils. Users also lose some sense of smell.
7. Use of cocaine during **pregnancy** can cut off oxygen to the fetus, seriously endangering its health. Doctors also report that the drug negatively affects the reproductive systems of men and women.

TF True or False?

Young, healthy people do not have heart attacks.

False. Although it is not common, young people can have heart attacks for any number of reasons. Witness the case of singer Karen Carpenter, who died of a heart attack related to her battle with anorexia. And Len Bias, a basketball player whose heart failure stemmed from his use of cocaine. In fact, cocaine is responsible for a large portion of heart attacks among young people—people in their teens.

Fact: *Not until the recent epidemic of cocaine-related deaths and health problems did society believe the drug was harmful. In fact, Sigmund Freud used cocaine—until he realized that it was addictive. Now, the United States government estimates that thirty million Americans have tried cocaine at least once; five million are regular users.*

Q. What is crack?

A. It's a solidified form of cocaine that is smoked, rather than sniffed or injected. Crack's effect on the body is like that of other forms of cocaine, but its "high" is even more intense and addictive. Unlike other cocaines, however, crack is relatively inexpensive, about twenty-five dollars for a fingernail-size "rock." This all adds up to one big problem: People who otherwise might not be able to afford drugs *can* buy crack. And because it is so addictive, users often feel desperate for more. Not only does their strong desire for the drug cause them to commit crimes (stealing money for more, assaulting people who "get in the way"), but crack's effect on the brain also results in other irrational behavior. You can probably verify this just by watching the news on TV!

Q. *What is "crashing"?*

A. This term refers to the withdrawal symptoms that cocaine users experience as they "come down" from a high. Cocaine produces extreme euphoria but what goes up, must come down, and cocaine brings you down hard. In fact, a recent survey of 500 cocaine abusers showed eighty-three percent suffer from depression.

Narcotics

Some narcotics are manufactured (such as methadone and meperidine) but most of the ones discussed here—opium, morphine, codeine, and heroin—are derived from a blossom called the Asian poppy. Doctors prescribe some of these drugs to relieve pain, but they are more often associated with illicit use and have a high potential for abuse.

Short-term effects: When these drugs are first injected, they may produce a strong "rushing" sensation, but later they make the user feel very relaxed. Users also experience drowsiness, clouded thinking, restlessness, nausea, and vomiting. Meanwhile, the heart rate is probably slower, the pupils are constricted, and breathing is shallow.

Long-term effects: People who use a lot of these drugs for a long time usually become dependent on them. Narcotics are expensive and users often find it difficult to get enough of them to achieve the desired effect. Withdrawal symptoms are painful (abdominal cramps, diarrhea, chills, sweating, nausea) and last a week or so. Prolonged users are also at risk for infections of the heart, skin disorders, and congested lungs.

Other dangers: Large doses can result in small pupils and cold, moist, discolored skin. Overdosing drastically slows down the breathing; the user may fall asleep and die. Infections from dirty needles, syringes, and solutions can lead to hepatitis, tetanus, liver disease, and AIDS. (See "AIDS and the Needle," page 90.) Malnutrition is another common health problem among narcotic users. Pregnant women who take these drugs—even in normal, prescribed amounts—are risking their babies' health and lives.

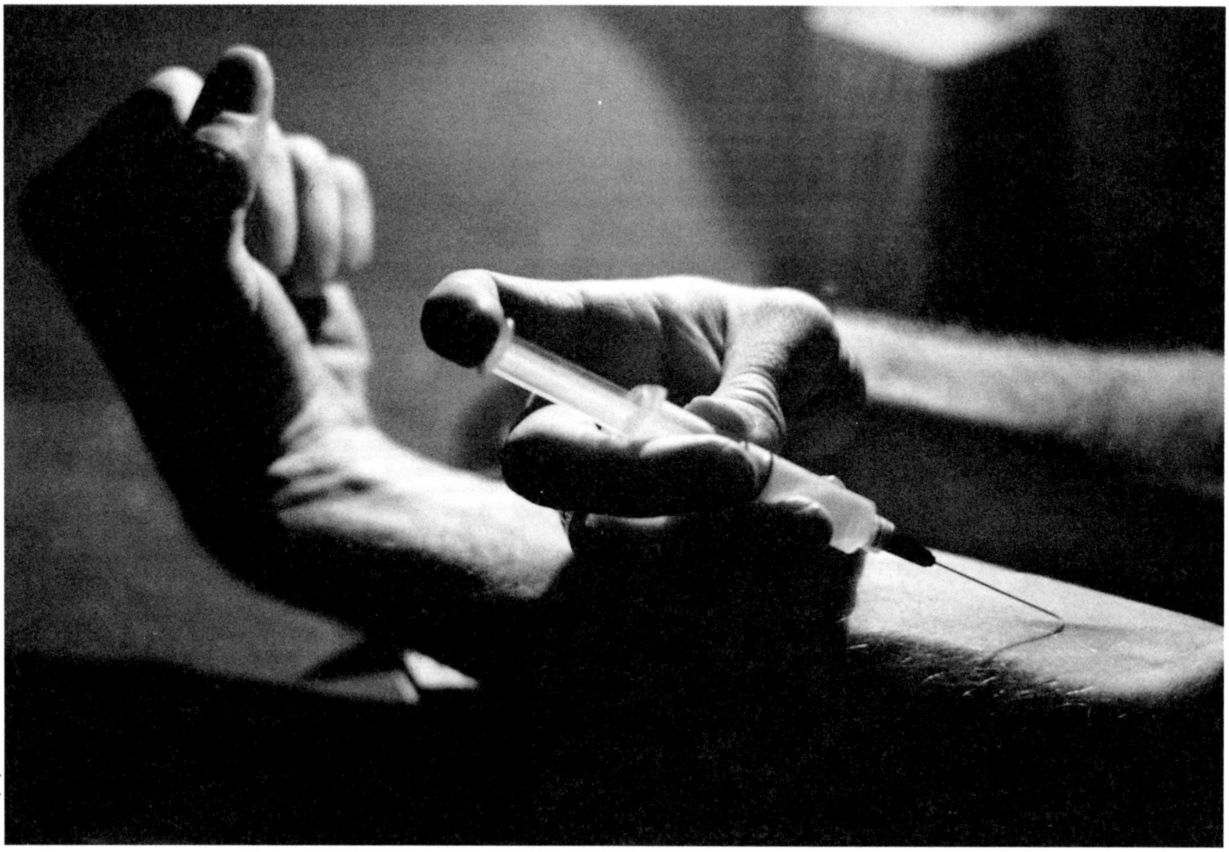

© Jeffrey Sylvester/FPG International

Substance abuse is not a problem unique to the late twentieth century. A hundred years ago, opium addicts collected in opium dens; today, heroin addicts collect in ''shooting galleries'' and crack addicts gather in crack dens in much the same way.

How a Few Narcotics Differ

Codeine: This drug is probably the weakest narcotic. In fact, you've probably taken codeine yourself—in cough medicine. Yet, codeine is dangerous when it's abused.

Heroin: In the United States, heroin is illegal because it's extremely addictive and powerful. Its main danger is overdose; because the effects last three to six hours, heroin users have to keep up injections (or sometimes inhaling) in order to avoid withdrawal discomfort. If the dose is too high, the user dies from respiratory failure.

Methadone: This laboratory-made substance is sometimes offered to heroin addicts in United States drug programs. It helps them deal with the withdrawal symptoms and gradually return to a drug-free world. Methadone is also addictive, but its prescription is carefully monitored.

Morphine: A strong painkiller, morphine is a widely used prescription drug. Some people get addicted to it during an illness or serious health problems because it works on the central nervous system and makes them unaware of pain. For some people, it also produces euphoria.

Opium: Morphine and codeine can be extracted from opium, a natural product of the poppy flower mentioned above. This drug may be smoked or sniffed.

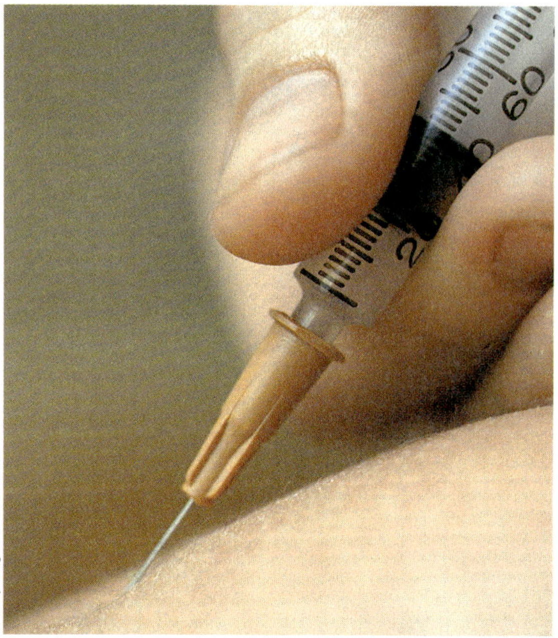

© Terry Qing/FPG International

AIDS and the Needle

Morphine, heroin, methadone, meperidine, barbiturates, amphetamines, and a few other drugs are injected, which means their users rely on syringes and needles. This in itself causes all sorts of health risks. For example, drug users who inject drugs with needles can seriously damage their veins, even though they may inject themselves in a new place each time.

What's more, there's always the chance that they'll use an infected needle. If people didn't share their needles and syringes, this wouldn't happen as often. But when a person is addicted to a drug, they feel a need to get it into their bodies quickly, and thus, will end up compromising their sanitary habits by borrowing a needle or using what's at hand. The bloodstream travels all over the body, so when germs, bacteria, or a virus are fed directly to a vessel, the disease risk is high. Liver disease, hepatitis, and tetanus were once the main dirty-needle risks, but during the last few years, the AIDS virus has become the biggest health concern.

AIDS stands for Acquired Immune Deficiency Syndrome, and is passed through contact of one person's bodily fluids to another's. It attacks the immune system, lowering an individual's resistance to disease. Sexual contact and sharing needles are the primary ways the virus is spread. At first, male homosexuals were at highest risk, but heterosexual intravenous drug users seem to be catching up. Because the needle makes direct contact with the primary bodily fluid—blood—drug-users are playing with their lives at even greater odds. (See "Human Sexuality.")

Hallucinogens

These illegal drugs produce both auditory and visual hallucinations (altered perceptions of reality). Hallucinogens include the drugs LSD (lysergic acid diethylamide), PCP (phencyclohexylpiperidine), and the plant-derived substances peyote, mescaline, and psilocybin.

Short-term effects: Hallucinogens affect people in different ways, depending on their mental states. Some users experience strong mood swings from joy to depression. These drugs are often taken because people desire an ''experience''—they feel that they can explore their minds and be more creative.

Long-term effects: Tolerance develops with frequent use so that users have to use more of the drug to achieve the desired effect. Physical dependence does not occur, nor do withdrawal symptoms.

Other dangers: Although hallucinogens haven't been linked with physical dependence, they're still very dangerous. Due to the nature of these drugs, users' perceptions of the ''real world'' are distorted and unrealistic. PCP use results in psychotic (insane or violent) behavior, putting other people at risk. Just as it is with taking any foreign substance into the body, an overdose could produce health-threatening symptoms or death.

How a Few Hallucinogens Differ

LSD: Produced in a chemical laboratory as a liquid or powder, LSD effects last about six to twelve hours and cause changes in body temperature, heart rate, blood pressure, perspiration, and can cause chills and goose pimples. A ''bad trip'' produces panic, anxiety, and paranoia.

Peyote and mescaline: These oral substances come from a cactus plant and are ingested orally. The hallucinations from the drugs initially include lights, animals, and geometric designs. These drugs may also induce panic states and anxiety.

PCP: Manufactured as a pill or powder, PCP is swallowed, smoked, sniffed, or even injected. PCP is much more powerful than LSD, peyote, or mescaline, and thus is more dangerous. For one reason, it's completely unpredictable; it may cause its user to react violently or drowsily, and it doesn't matter if the person has tried the drug one time or twenty times. Sometimes PCP is sprinkled on marijuana to achieve a more intense high.

Q. *Why do a lot of celebrities seem to take drugs?*

A. Athletes, music stars, actors, and other performers say they're under a lot of pressure and need these substances to help them relax and cope with their problems. Drugs can only cause them more problems. How many times have you heard about celebrities getting "busted" for possession? Ever notice how many have overcome their drug problems and tell stories about the hard times they went through? Sadder still, how many famous people can you name who've died in a drug accident or overdose? You'll probably be able to name ten with no effort. But the fact is these people live in a fishbowl, of sorts, and the media loves to make a big story of their drug habits or their recovery. There are a lot of other people with all kinds of jobs who have drug problems, we just never hear about them.

Janis Joplin, a popular singer in the 1960s, died of a drug overdose. Many celebrities, though very popular and successful, mistakenly think that drugs or alcohol can replace the euphoria they feel when they perform or take away feelings of loneliness, insecurity, or depression.

Marijuana and Hashish

How does marijuana fit into the four major drug groups? It acts partly as a depressant and partly as a stimulant, depending on the dose and the individual. Marijuana comes from a common plant with the biological name of *Cannibis sativa* and is usually dried and chopped up like tobacco and smoked. Sometimes, it's eaten. Marijuana comes from the leaves; hashish comes from the flowering tops.

Short-term effects: Like most drugs, marijuana increases blood pressure and heart rate. At the same time, it lowers blood sugar and body temperature; dilates blood vessels in the eyes (thus causing bloodshot eyes); and causes a dry throat and mouth. Some people feel giddy and talkative while smoking pot; others get quiet. In any case, thinking is slower and short-term memory is impaired, which means that a person high on marijuana could read a book and not remember it.

Long-term effects: The health risks of marijuana use are different from those of most other drugs. Some examples:

- Like smoking tobacco, smoking marijuana over a long period of time can cause cancer of the lungs and other parts of the body. Users also show signs of other lung problems characteristic of tobacco abusers. In fact, marijuana smoke may be even more damaging, since it's held in the lungs for longer than cigarette smoke. (See "Tobacco: Long-term Losses," page 35.)
- The reproductive system is also affected by marijuana. Not only has the fertility of females and males been shown to be impaired, babies born to a female pot-smoker are likely to suffer symptoms similar to fetal alcohol syndrome (see page 60).
- Marijuana affects the heart, too, by increasing the heart rate. This can cause chest pains and very low blood pressure in people with heart problems.
- Some studies suggest that use of marijuana reduces an individual's immunity to disease.
- Researchers have found that prolonged use of marijuana causes "burnout," or dull thinking, slowness, and confusion. It's also clear this drug affects the memory. Doctors suspect these symptoms are a result of brain damage by marijuana.

Interestingly, marijuana is not addictive for everyone; there are no physical withdrawal symptoms. However, one can be psychologically dependent on it. This means that marijuana abusers think they need to smoke for a sense of well-being, and the drug becomes a very important part of their lives.

Other dangers: Because marijuana affects one's concentration and timing, driving under its influence is very risky. Doctors are also concerned that pot-smoking young people, who are not yet developed sexually, physically, or mentally, will have problems growing to their full potential. (See "Human Sexuality.")

TF True or False?

Tobacco and marijuana have always been thought to be very unhealthy substances.

False. If you've read "Tobacco: Old Habits Die Hard" (page 21), you know that doctors didn't nail down tobacco's ill effects until the 1950s. Today, doctors are finding out more about the effects of marijuana. Although the consequences are already threatening, researchers may discover even more bad news.

Q. What is polydrug abuse?

A. Poly, meaning "many," is the serious addiction to two or more drugs. Marijuana, alcohol, cocaine, and tranquilizers are the most common drugs that are mixed. As you can imagine, the consequences of taking more than one drug are even more serious than taking just one. For example, when a person smokes marijuana, her body is partially limited in its ability to eliminate certain toxins. When she drinks alcohol, its toxins build up in the bloodstream and organs. Mixing barbiturates and alcohol is also dangerous.

Here's something else you should know: Drug users who get sick and are brought into the emergency room are at high risk to suffer serious consequences because doctors have a hard time figuring out their symptoms. One drug may complicate the tell-tale signs of another.

How a Drug Habit Forms

Throughout the preceding pages, you've read several references to "physical dependence," "psychological dependence," "tolerance," and "addiction." What do they mean?

When people first begin to take drugs, they don't usually go for a large dose. At first, a small amount—a few drags on a marijuana joint, a tiny bit of barbiturate or amphetamine—has a tremendous effect. As a person takes the drug more on a regular basis, her body may develop a tolerance. The first time you go out in the sun in April, for example, you might get a sunburn. But by the middle or end of the summer, you're probably less likely to get burned because your skin has already been exposed to the sun many times; it has developed a tolerance. (For health information on sunbathing, see "Maintaining Good Health.") With drugs, a similar thing happens, so the user has to increase her dose in order to get the same "high."

If she continues to take large doses for a long time—perhaps weeks or months—she may become physically dependent on the drug. This means her body has gotten so used to the drug, the body *needs* it. When she stops taking the drug or drastically cuts back her dosage, the body will answer with withdrawal symptoms. Trembling, hallucinations, nausea, and vomiting are typical withdrawal symptoms, but sometimes they're more or less severe, depending on the drug and the level of addiction. The withdrawal symptoms will disappear after a certain time, but some users have trouble outlasting them.

Some drugs can cause their users to be psychologically dependent, too. This means the individual "needs" the drug emotionally; otherwise, she can't be happy or satisfied. The drug has become a very important part of her life. She's addicted.

There's Much More to It Than That

Have you ever tried to tell anybody about hundreds of chemicals in a few pages? It's not easy, so don't think what you've read is the whole story. There are effects that weren't thoroughly discussed and plenty of drugs that weren't even mentioned. What's more, researchers learn more about drug abuse everyday. In order to get all this new information to you, we would have to add a new page to this book every month.

Even so, what you've just read should help you understand what's out there. If you have any questions, don't hesitate to ask them. Read Part II for where to get more information.

P A R T I I :

How Can I Avoid Or, If I Have To, Handle Substance Abuse?

You can go out of your way to avoid cigarettes, alcohol, and nonmedical drugs but you'll probably be confronted with them sooner or later. Maybe you'll walk into the girls' bathroom tomorrow and see your best friend smoking cigarettes. Or perhaps ten years from now you'll find out your brother is using cocaine. Maybe you'll even develop a problem yourself.

At this point then, you'll want to know everyday tactics for dealing with this health risk. The first strategy is to avoid them completely. Easier said than done? Then you'll be glad to read our tips for saying no and handling peer pressure. Some people aren't good at avoiding the problem, so there's also information on helping a friend out of trouble—and even yourself.

Finally, because the problem of substance abuse often requires detailed attention, we provide you with more sources of information. By all means, if you or someone you know is abusing a substance, don't be too shy or embarrassed to get help. You're not alone; that's what these agencies were created for, so take advantage of them.

© Joe McNally/Wheeler Pictures

Some people do drugs or drink alcohol as an act of rebellion. It's one of the best ways they know to challenge "the establishment." Teens sometimes take drugs as an act of independence.

Avoid These Substances Whenever Possible

The decision as to whether or not you try alcohol, tobacco, or drugs is yours; we wouldn't try to tell you anything else. What we can do is tell you the facts—which is what we did in Part I—and then give you steps for the safest route to take.

After taking into account all the short-term gains and the long-term losses, you've probably decided that avoiding these substances is smart. On your own paper, list ten reasons why you should avoid drugs. Here are some of ours:

1. You need "your wits about you" in order to perform well in school; the use of most of these substances limits your abilities.
2. By avoiding alcohol and nonmedical drugs, you can count on not making a fool of yourself with a date or someone you want to impress.
3. Drugs or alcohol change the "real you" into someone else. By avoiding them, you can be sure your friends like you for who you are.
4. Life has enough risks without adding a health risk to it.
5. These substances can get you in trouble with parents, teachers, and sometimes the law. By

© Peter Menzel/Wheeler Pictures

Often, an individual or small group will use a substance to feel special or to create an image. Just as you might get a new haircut to surprise your parents, some people take drugs to get attention and recognition from others.

avoiding them, you avoid trouble.

6. If you begin using drugs, alcohol, or tobacco products now while you're developing your adult personality, they'll be harder to kick later, since you'll have spent some important developmental years using them.
7. Smoking cigarettes, drinking alcohol, or taking drugs doesn't fit in with the "image" you have of yourself.
8. Avoiding substance abuse takes more "guts" than trying them.
9. You don't want to set a bad example for little kids.
10. You're simply not interested in them.

What reasons did you come up with? Do you agree or disagree with any of the reasons listed above? It's okay if your reasons are nothing like ours. In order to make a plan work (like passing up marijuana or kicking a cigarette habit), you have to decide for yourself what good reasons are. Then, you'll be convinced that this is the right thing to do.

What if you *aren't* convinced that avoiding drugs is the best thing for you? Then write ten reasons why you don't think you should avoid these substances. Compare this list with your previous one. How do they differ?

How to Say "No"

It's easy to get caught off-guard. You can be with a bunch of friends, laughing and having a good time, when all of the sudden, someone hands you a joint. These kinds of situations are tricky, all right, and it takes savvy to handle them. One way is to have a pat answer all ready before it happens. Practice one or two of these answers over and over again until the response seems almost automatic. When you find yourself in a difficult situation, you'll be surprised how much easier it will be to resist.

- "Thanks, but I want to remember this party."
- "Not tonight."
- "I'd rather have a soda."
- "I'll have a better time without it."
- "Thanks, but I better not. That stuff makes me really sick."
- "I really don't feel like it now, but thanks."
- "I guess I'll pass. I have to study tonight."
- "Better not. Coach is starting me first string tomorrow night."

You get the picture. These answers are good because they don't really insult anyone or make you look bad—just smooth. You've not only said no, but you have a good reason.

Sometimes though, a simple "no" or nice way of saying no doesn't work. Some people are pretty persistent about passing their habits on to others. What to do: This time, make it simple, but sincere. Say "no thanks," but look directly into the person's eyes and make sure your facial expression and tone really say "no." (Check yourself in the mirror. Sometimes, we don't realize how wishy-washy we sound or look.) You may have to repeat "no" a few times.

Here are other ways to deal with this problem. Maybe they fit your style better, or maybe you'll use a combination of things. The most important thing: Don't give in. It's your life and your decision. You'll lose more respect by backing down on your opinion at this point.

- Change the subject. Just as someone is about to insist that you take a drink of beer again, say something about Algebra II homework or last night's rock concert. Tell the person, "Look, I'm heading out to shoot a few baskets. You want to go?" Or, "Why don't you show me the shoes you bought for the prom?"
- Have something else to do. "No, I'm going to see what the guys are doing outside." Or, "No, I'm leaving in a minute."
- If a friend teases you about not participating, tease her back. Such as: "Oh, right, and you think *you* know how to have a good time? That's not what I heard."
- Don't socialize with people who use these substances. That might be the best way to avoid uncomfortable situations.

As you can see, some of these answers can simply delay the issue. That's fine for the time being, but you may have to "pass" on using these substances again. Eventually, you'll get tired of making excuses, and they'll realize how you really feel. If this is the case, you might want to pull each of your substance-abusing friends aside and explain to them that alcohol, tobacco, and drugs aren't your thing—and tell them why. Some friends will accept that; others won't. If somebody has a problem with what you choose to do with your life, the next move is yours. You can put up with them or stay away from them. It's hard to give up friends, but it's *your* health. You decide what's important.

Putting on the Pressure

Earlier in the book, you read about how and why teens are vulnerable to peer pressure. It can be very influential at times. Who hasn't been tempted to wear a certain kind of jacket or boots because "everybody else does"? Just about everyone gives into peer pressure at some time—no matter how old they are.

Don't kid yourself about how strong peer pressure can be. It's not as if other teens will walk up to you and say, "Here, take this coke, and you'll feel like a heel if you don't." Peer pressure is usually more subtle than that. Still, it helps to know that it's out there and to be able to recognize it. By practicing ways to say no, you'll be armed when the occasion rises. Even then, you'll probably have to do some smart thinking and talking. You can do it.

Other Ways to Get "High"

You don't need any more pep talks on how substance abuse produces short-term gains with long-term losses. What you might not have heard is that substances make artificial highs. Have you ever tried a natural high? Sure, you have. Maybe it was when your girlfriend first looked at you. Or when you won a contest. Or when your Dad took you deep-sea fishing. You can probably think of plenty of other examples.

One kind of natural high has been in the news a lot lately. Have you ever heard of a "runner's high"? It's a euphoric, soaring feeling that makes some runners feel as if they could run forever. Other forms of exercise—dancing and ice skating, for example—also can create this natural high. Doctors think the high may be due to certain kinds of hormones that are released during exercise that stimulate good feelings.

On the other hand, another recent study may disprove this idea. When researchers at the University of Hawaii gave runners a drug to block the production of these hormones, they enjoyed running, anyway. So perhaps it's just the thrill of exercising. Who knows? Try it and see if it works for you. (See "Exercise.")

Passing Up the Passenger Seat

With so many statistics out about drunk driving, it may be hard to believe that people would actually get in a car with a drunk driver. People do it all the time. They wonder if the driver should be driving, but nobody else says anything and they don't want to make a scene.

It might be embarrassing, but you might have to insist that you won't ride with a drunk driver. Try reasoning first. If the driver rebels—as they frequently do—simply refuse to ride with her. Find someone else to ride with, call your parents to come pick you up, walk, take a bus—anything that's safer. Your friend might be mad at first, but perhaps when she's sober she'll understand. If she doesn't, then it's unfortunate she doesn't realize she's risking her life, yours and the lives of other people on the road. Maybe you can get this point across to her.

Here's an even trickier situation: What do you do if a parent or relative who has been drinking gets behind the wheel? Try the same technique; maybe it will work. Speak respectfully and honestly, citing the reasons why you don't want to ride with him. "Dad, don't be upset, but it might be best for Mom to drive home (or, I'd rather we walk home, take a taxi, etc.)." Or, try saying something like, "I know you don't think beer will hurt your driving skills, but I've read that alcohol is alcohol. It's only because I care, Dad. I don't want any of us to get hurt." You know your parents and what approach might work best. Don't be embarrassed. You might save somebody's life. (See also "Students Against Drunk Driving" page 103.)

© Bob Peterson/FPG International

Research suggests that endorphins—a special kind of hormone in the body—are stimulated whenever you get a good workout. A lot of people prefer this natural high to the unnatural one you get from substance abuse.

Students Against Drunk Driving

In 1980, a thirteen-year-old girl named Cari Lightner was killed by a drunk driver. Her mother was understandably upset, but she did more than cry. She started an organization called Mothers Against Drunk Drivers (M.A.D.D.) to educate the public about drunk driving, fight for proper punishment for offenders, and help the victims of drunk-driver accidents. Today, the organization has members all over the country.

Young people started a spin-off of this club called Students Against Drunk Driving (S.A.D.D.). Teens in this national organization sign S.A.D.D. contracts with their parents, promising to call home for a ride when they can't get a sober driver. The parents promise not to ask any questions or to get mad, no matter what the time or circumstances—or at least, until the next day. The important thing is to get home safely, and not to be discouraged from calling.

Does this sound like a good idea to you? You can follow these guidelines without actually having a S.A.D.D. contract. However, if you're interested in this organization, write to: Students Against Drunk Driving, W.T. Woodson High School, 9525 Main Street, Fairfax, Virginia 22032.

© Gerard Fritz/FPG International

Dealing with Passive Smokers

Have you ever had a smoker ask, "Do you mind if I smoke?" How did you answer?

More and more, smokers are asking if you "mind" their cigarettes. This is the polite and correct thing to do. Studies show that passive smoking is very unhealthy, and the law is already reacting to this research. (See "Passive Smoking," page 43.) Many public places do not permit smoking at all, or they're divided into "No Smoking" and "Smoking" sections. This way, everyone's happy. When smokers aren't separated from nonsmokers, you could be subjected to a health risk.

If someone is kind enough to ask your permission to smoke, be nice right back, but honest. "I'd rather you didn't. But I do appreciate your asking." If more smokers and nonsmokers were decent about this, it wouldn't be a problem.

Don't keep quiet when a smoker is wrong. You have your rights. This is especially true in a designated "No Smoking" area. If a smoker lights up in an elevator or on the wrong side of the theater or restaurant, try this: "Excuse me. Would you please put your cigarette out? There isn't supposed to be smoking here and it bothers me."

At this point, you'll have to see what happens and judge what to do next. If the smoker puts the cigarette out, thank him. Say something nice, like "I wish all smokers were as considerate." Then, the smoker is likely to think before he does it again.

If the smoker gets mad or says something rude, you can try to reason with him. "Sir, I'm not telling you to not smoke at all. There's a smoking area in the balcony; maybe you'd be more comfortable there." Or, "I'm only trying to follow rules and stay healthy. Once you're outside you can smoke all you want to."

If all else fails, you can report the smoker to someone who's in charge, like the theater or restaurant manager or building superintendent. It's unfortunate that some adults don't act very mature, but at least you can.

Don't Get Caught

The TV movie about teenage suicide had Carrie wiping away tears. She thought it was so sweet the way the two young lovers died together! Although the movie was followed with startling statistics about suicides, she couldn't help but think maybe that was the answer for her and her boyfriend Brad. (See "Stress and Mental Health.")

Ron's eyes were glued to the page. While the book he was reading made it clear that sex posed too many problems for teens, it only made him more curious. Why were adults going to so much trouble to keep young people from trying sex? He was dying to find out what it was like. (See "Human Sexuality.")

Don't do it. Don't get caught in an "information trap." When this happens, people get "turned on" by news that's supposed to help, not hurt, a problem. For example, health experts have been very concerned about recent movies and news stories about teenage suicide; they're afraid they give ideas to young people. Sure enough, one suicide case is often followed by a slew of other deaths. The police also worry about this phenomenon, since one news story about an unusual crime can inspire other criminals to do the same.

Similarly, after reading all the details of alcohol, drugs, and cigarettes, you might have been even more curious about what it's like to try them. That's reasonable; most people would. But don't overestimate the short-term gains and underestimate the long-term losses. You don't want to be guilty of "tunnel vision" and ignore the risks you'll take. Don't get caught dead.

©Carolyn A. McKeone/FPG International

Some kids will only try a drug once or twice. Then they decide that they don't like the way it makes them feel, and they don't like the possibility of getting caught.

Take Steps to Correct a Problem

You've read a lot of bad news about alcohol, tobacco, and drugs. The good news is that in many cases, the unhealthy effects can be reversed. For example, smokers who stop smoking have a good chance of clearing up their lungs and reducing heart disease. The liver of an alcoholic can improve after the abuser stops drinking. And drug addicts can nix the risk of overdoses and other accidents by stopping their dependence in time.

A substance abuser *can* kick the habit, but it takes work. Here's one plan. The person should:

1. Face the problem and come to terms with the fact that he or she needs help. Otherwise, the attempt is a waste of time. A look at the pluses and minuses of the habit will probably get the abuser in the right frame of mind for this first step.
2. Make a list of reasons for quitting. Begin a healthy living program, including sleep, nutrition, and exercise. People who feel good want to feel even better.
3. Choose the method for quitting. See pages 98–100 for a few ideas.
4. Select a specific day to quit. The sooner the better.
5. Stick to the date.
6. Reinforce the decision. Use substitutes for the missing drug: nibble on carrots instead of smoking, drink seltzer water instead of alcohol. Re-read the lists of quitting reasons from time to time. Plan frequent rewards and celebrate anniversaries of the quitting date—a week, month, year, etc.

Signs that Someone's in Trouble

Maybe it's Dad, or your brother, or your best friend, even yourself, but if someone near you abuses a substance, you probably suspect it already. Here are tell-tale symptoms. A person doesn't have to have all in order to have a problem—just one or a few.

For drinking:

- Drinking everyday, or almost everyday, even if it's only one or two drinks
- Family, school, or work problems caused by drinking
- An inability to know when to stop drinking
- "Blackouts" or forgetting what happened during intoxication
- Getting drunk frequently
- Starting the day with a drink
- A need to drink increasing amounts of alcohol to achieve the desired effect
- Breaking the law while intoxicated
- Feeling uncomfortable when alcohol is not available
- Marked changes in personality or behavior when drinking
- Drinking alone or secretively

For Drugs:

- Taking any illicit drugs
- A change in work or school performance
- Borrowing money
- Rebelling against discipline or criticism
- Sneaking around or hiding things
- Treating friends and family differently
- "Flying off the handle" frequently
- A change in mood or attitude
- Ignoring rules or deadlines
- Making new friends, especially with drug users
- Shifts from depression to euphoria

For Tobacco:

- Any use

© Peter Menzel/Wheeler Pictures

Help for Smokers

About twenty million smokers try to quit every year, but only one million manage to quit for good. Why? You could say they don't have willpower, but most addictions are more complicated than that. Doctors believe we should not underestimate the power of nicotine as an addictive drug.

The six steps on page 106 are designed to help people stop any substance abuse, but here are more helpful hints:

- Visit the dentist and have your teeth cleaned when you quit smoking. Because tobacco stains will be gone, you might feel reluctant to "mess them up again" with a cigarette.
- Talk with other ex-smokers for support. They'll be more sympathetic.
- Avoid situations where other people are likely to smoke. The temptation to join them could be too strong.
- Warn family and friends that you're going to stop smoking and that you'll be "edgy" and need support.
- Think of different things to do to replace cigarettes: Chew sugarless gum to keep your mouth busy. Take a shower for relaxation. Exercise. Snap rubber bands. Develop a new hobby.

The Support System

Experts say that one of the keys to a successful smoking cessation plan is support from family and friends. Encouragement is important, so some ex-smoker candidates work out a deal with a "support person." This could be a friend, wife, husband, or even a daughter or son. (Perhaps you could help your parents this way.) The idea is for the person to "back" the smoker without nagging. Here are some guidelines:

- Ask the smoker what would be helpful. Realize that the first few nonsmoking days are tough, so the smoker may be aggravated easily. Perhaps the support person could help eliminate stress by answering the phone, helping with housework, and so on.
- Praise is acceptable, but lectures and scolding are not. It's the difference between complimenting someone for not smoking and commenting if the smoker slips and has a cigarette.
- A reward system might help. Tell your friend or family member that you'll wash her car, do all the laundry, cook dinner, or treat her to a movie, if she makes it through the first week without a cigarette. The following week, find something else that makes a good reward.
- When the would-be ex-smoker is tempted to have a cigarette, remind her of all the reasons she chose for not smoking. Be positive; stress the benefits of quitting, such as saving money and getting rid of bad breath.
- If the person does have a cigarette, don't give up. Help the smoker examine how and why the mistake happened, and think of ways to prevent the reoccurrence of a similar situation. For example, if your brother relapsed and had a cigarette with his morning coffee, you could suggest that he have a bagel instead.

A Smoker's Contract

Sometimes, a written contract between a smoker and a "support person" help. Try this and see.

Contract to Quit Smoking

I, ________(your name)________, make the promise to myself that I will quit smoking cigarettes on ______(date)______. I am doing this for these reasons:

____

____

____

____

Date________(date you signed the contract)________

Signed________(your signature)________

Contract For the Smoker's Support Person

I, ________(your name)________, make the promise to give helpful (but not critical) advice and support to ________(smoker's name)________ in his/her efforts to quit smoking. I agree to be a positive and understanding friend during this time.

Date________(date you signed the contract)________

Signed________(your signature)________

Other Stop-Smoking Approaches

Researchers know that smoking is a tough habit to break and are constantly looking for new ways to help. One method that has had some success is nicotine gum. Although some people claim that smokers aren't satisfied with getting their "nicotine fix" this way and complain about unpleasant side effects (stomach ache, indigestion, bad taste), some doctors believe it works when smokers follow the prescription. By starting off with several pieces of high-level nicotine gum during the first weeks, and tapering off to smaller doses, some smokers are able to beat their addiction.

Besides gum, people are also experimenting with the success of hypnosis; acupuncture (a Chinese practice of using needles to cure diseases and health problems); aversion therapy (the association of unpleasant feelings with cigarettes, achieved in different ways: electric shocks, drugs that make cigarettes taste bad, having smoke blown at an individual, and so on); and arm patches (a special strip that regularly releases a dose of nicotine into a small opening in the arm). However, none of these methods has been proven 100 percent effective. In addition, slews of books, video tapes, and stop-smoking groups are available, some with limited success.

Stop-smoking groups enjoy some success since the support is constant and group meetings encourage smokers to talk about their problems. The American Cancer Society runs special campaigns and clinics every year, usually for no charge or a small fee. For more information, look for your town's local chapter in the phone directory, or write:

American Cancer Society
19 West 56th Street
New York, NY 10019

Other places to write for more information:

Office on Smoking and Health
Technical Information Center
Park Building, Room 116
5600 Fishers Lane
Rockville, MD 20857

American Heart Association
7320 Greenville Avenue
Dallas, TX 75231

National Clearinghouse for Smoking and Health
Westwood Towers, Room 500
5401 Westbard Avenue
Bethesda, MD 20016

American Lung Association
1740 Broadway
New York, NY 10019

© Marv Wolf/FPG International

Ask around and you'll find out that many people know someone who was killed or injured by a drunk driver. The number of drunk driving incidents that occur today is scary and outrageous.

Help for Alcoholics

The earlier problem drinkers get treatment, the better their odds for success. Doctors believe that fifty to seventy five percent of people who try to beat alcohol are successful. Before anything can happen, an alcoholic has to realize he or she has a problem. This may be where you come in. If you want to help someone with a drinking problem, it's unlikely that he'll ever confront it—unless you say something.

Generally, it's accepted that alcoholics can't kick the habit on their own. Some do, but the going is rough. Yet, it's easy to contact health professionals and counselors in your community and get the answers and guidance you need, whether you're the one with the drinking problem, or someone you know is. Here are some ideas:

- Call someone who is close at hand: your doctor, school counselor, clergyman, local hospitals, mental health centers, and county health department. All of these resources are likely to have information or insight into alcoholism.
- Check the telephone directory yellow pages under "Information and Referral," "Alcoholism," "Alcoholism Treatment," "Mental Health." You'll probably find a few different offices that can answer your questions. You don't necessarily have to go in and identify yourself. Try calling and asking questions first, such as: "Can you help me? I'm thirteen, I think I have a drinking problem (or, my mom has a drinking problem), and I don't know exactly what to do about it." Chances are, they'll answer your specific questions, give you a little advice, and then refer you to an alcoholism program.
- If you have trouble figuring out who's the best person to call for your particular problem, or if there is no special service of this nature in your town, contact your state department of alcoholism services. Every state has one, but their names vary. Look in your telephone directory under "State Government" listings and you'll probably find one. Or contact:

  National Association of State Alcohol and Drug Abuse Directors
  444 N. Capitol Street, N.W.
  Suite 530
  Washington, D.C. 20001
  (202) 783-6868

  National Clearinghouse for Alcohol Information
  P.O. Box 2345
  Rockville, MD 20852
  (301) 468-2600

  National Council on Alcoholism
  12 W. 21st Street
  New York, NY 10010
- This famous organization helps anyone who wants to overcome his or her drinking problem. Look under "Alcoholics Anonymous" in your telephone directory for the local group, or write to this address to help you find a nearby group:
  AA
  P.O. Box 459
  Grand Central Station
  New York, NY 10163
  (212) 686-1100
- Because health experts know that teens are concerned about and affected by alcoholic family and friends, they created a group that helps. Alateen is part of Al-Anon, an organization for relatives of problem drinkers. Alateen will help you cope. Look under "Alateen" or "Al-Anon" in the phone directory, or write:
  Al-Anon Family Group Headquarters
  P.O. Box 182
  New York, NY 10159-0182
  (212) 683-1771

Do's and Don'ts for Friends and Family of an Alcoholic

- *Don't* wait for someone to get drunk one more time before you confront the problem. Do it now.
- *Do* get help from an organization like Alateen or Al-Anon.
- *Don't* cover up someone's drinking problem or protect him or her from the truth.
- *Do* let the problem drinker know that you're learning about alcoholism through books, magazines, a school program, Alateen, or other sources.
- *Don't* nag or scold the drinker.
- *Do* try to remain calm, unemotional, and honest when you're speaking to the alcoholic about his problem.
- *Don't* argue with an alcoholic when he's drunk.
- *Do* be patient and keep on trying whenever you fail.
- *Don't* keep ''checking'' on an alcoholic.
- *Do* give yourself a break; get out and have a good time and relieve pressure.
- *Don't* get in the car with a drunk driver.
- *Do* encourage new activities and interests for the problem drinker.
- *Don't* blame yourself.

© J. Pickerell/FPG International

Help for Drug Abusers

Treatment for drug abuse may be most difficult of all. Many times, users don't seek help until they overdose, reach the brink of death, or create a family crisis. Because some drugs are highly addictive, physically and psychologically, outside help is necessary. Even after the initial habit is kicked, drug abusers need help to rebuild their daily lives.

Drug organizations are much like alcoholic groups. Here are some you can contact. First, see if you have a local chapter listed in your phone directory. Check the yellow pages under "Drug Abuse" or "Mental Health" as well. Crisis center staff members are also trained to help people with drug problems; look in the yellow or white pages for these organizations. If you can't find one, they're often listed under "Suicide Prevention," "Crime Victims," "Abuse." Hospitals often have special programs for drug problems, too.

If all this doesn't work, these national offices will steer you in the right direction.

Alcohol, Drug Abuse, and Mental Health Administration
5600 Fishers Lane
Rockville, MD 20857
(301) 443-4883

National Institute on Drug Abuse
11400 Rockville Pike
Room 110
Rockville, MD 20852

Drug Abuse Prevention (a toll-free hotline)
1-800-638-2045
In Maryland: 1-800-492-6605

Narcotics Anonymous
16155 Wyandotte Street
Van Nuys, CA
(818) 780-3951

National Clearinghouse for Drug Abuse Information
P.O. Box 416
Dept. DQ
Kensington, MD 20795
(301) 443-6500

ending a Hand to Drug Abusers

The philosophy behind supporting a person with drug problems is similar to that of helping smokers and alcoholics (check our lists on page 108 and 111). Don't nag. Be positive. Be understanding. Get more information. Help when you can. If you can get someone to seek treatment, that's great! But even after the person has kicked the habit, you'll need to be there. It takes time and patience—he won't get everything back to normal for some time.

Don't let someone else's problem ruin your life. If a drug user doesn't want or won't accept help, there isn't much you can do but try again—and even that might not work. Do what you can, but take care of yourself, too. As a teen on the brink of adulthood, you've got your own health concerns. Stress from everyday living is trying enough without letting someone else pile *his* problems on you. If you need it, get outside help for dealing with this stress, and you'll be in better shape to help your sick friend or family member. You'll not only be doing your friend a favor, you'll be helping society.

Alcoholics Anonymous was established in 1934; many people feel it is the most effective way ever found to help problem drinkers.

GLOSSARY

Addiction A great need for something—to the point that to stop the activity is very difficult and the response to cessation is uncomfortable. For example, one can be addicted to shopping, to caffeine, or to a drug.

Adrenal glands A pair of organs that are located above the kidneys and make hormones.

AIDS Acquired Immune Deficiency Syndrome—a sexually transmitted disease. See Human Sexuality.

Alcohol There are two kinds of alcohol: One kind is made from the chemical ethyl and is used as a skin cleaner; the other kind is a drink, such as beer or whiskey, made by brewing sugar with yeast.

Alcoholics Anonymous A worldwide group, founded in 1935, whose members are alcoholics who no longer drink. The purpose is to help each other stop drinking and stay sober.

Alcoholism An extreme dependence on alcohol.

Amphetamines A group of drugs that stimulate the nervous system. Doctors sometimes prescribe amphetamines for certain disorders. However, people abuse the drugs because amphetamines make them feel "up," not tired. The effects of amphetamines can backfire and cause severe paranoia.

Anesthesia The inability to feel pain. This condition is brought on by certain drugs, usually when you have surgery or other medical treatments.

Anxiety An uneasiness or fearful concern about something. For example, you might feel anxious about meeting your Mom's new boyfriend, or you might feel anxious over a long period of time without really knowing why.

Aorta The main vessel of the heart.

Auditory Having to do with hearing. For example, the auditory piece on your telephone is the part you hear with.

Barbiturates A group of drugs that act as sedatives or make their users feel sleepy. Use of large amounts of barbiturates slows down breathing and could cause a coma or death.

Breathing tract Windpipe—the passage for the breath from the larynx to the lungs. Also known as the trachea.

Bladder The sac that holds your urine.

Bronchial tubes Air passages within the lungs.

Bronchitis An illness that involves the swelling of the lung membranes. Bronchitis may be caused by a viral infection or by breathing in substances that weaken the lungs and make them susceptible to infection. Cigarette

GLOSSARY

smoking and air pollution, for example, are linked to bronchitis.

Carbon dioxide A clear, odorless gas found in nature. When you breathe in, you breathe oxygen. But when you breathe out, you release carbon dioxide.

Carbon monoxide A clear, odorless, poisonous gas made when carbon or other fuel is burned. A car engine, for example, makes carbon monoxide.

Carcinogen A substance that can cause the growth of cancer.

Central nervous system The main network of coordination and control for the entire body. The central nervous system is made up of the brain and the spine.

Cervix The lower part of the uterus in a female. See Human Sexuality.

Chemical compound A combination of chemicals that acts as one chemical.

Cilia Tiny, hairlike structures that line the body's windpipe and lungs. The job of the cilia is to "sweep" foreign substances—such as smoke or air pollution—from the lungs.

Cirrhosis A disease of the liver.

Cocaine A drug that is illegal unless it is used by a doctor under specific guidelines. Cocaine can be sniffed, injected, smoked, and in a few cases, eaten.

Codeine A narcotic that reduces mild pain, treats diarrhea, and stops coughing. People have been known to become addicted to codeine.

Coma A state of deep unconsciousness. A person in a coma looks as if he or she is asleep—except he or she doesn't wake up for a long period of time. Comas may be caused by injury, brain tumors, or drug abuse, and they have been known to last for years.

Crack A form of cocaine.

Delirium A serious mental disorder, caused by a problem with brain functions. The symptoms include confusion, speech problems, anxiety, and abnormal excitement. Nutritional disorders or drug use can cause delirium. See Nutrition.

Delusion A strong belief that someone has that is not true. For example, if you were convinced that you were a cat, then you would be the victim of a delusion.

Depressant A substance that decreases the activity of the body. For example, alcohol is a depressant because it slows down your heart and brain functions.

Digestive system The organs and glands through which food passes. The mouth, throat, stomach, and small and large intestines are all part of the digestive system.

GLOSSARY

Distillation A process that turns solid substances into gas, and then gas into liquids. Some alcoholic drinks are made by distillation.

Emphysema A disease of the lungs. Emphysema can be hereditary, but a major cause is smoking.

Esophagus The digestive tube that leads from below the throat to the stomach.

Euphoria A super-good feeling. For example, you might feel euphoric immediately after winning an important contest.

Exhale To breathe out.

Fermentation A process that chemically alters a substance. For example, the juice of grapes ferment when they are allowed to sit for a long period of time under certain conditions. Fermentation helps turn grapes into wine.

Fetus An unborn baby.

Freebasing A special way of smoking cocaine with a water pipe.

Hallucinate To see objects or scenes that aren't really there. Users of some types of drugs hallucinate.

Hallucinogens A group of drugs that stimulate the brain. They are called hallucinogens because they sometimes cause their users to hallucinate (see above). Long-term use of hallucinogens has been linked to depression.

Hangover The physical effects of having drunk too much alcohol. Symptoms include nausea, dizziness, headache, and exhaustion.

Hashish A drug similar to marijuana, both of which come from varieties of the hemp plant.

Heart palpitations A pounding or racing of the heart.

Hepatitis A disease of the liver.

Heroin An illegal drug that can be sniffed or injected. Its effects last three to six hours. Once the user develops a physical dependence, he or she suffers from withdrawal symptoms after those three to six hours have passed. The symptoms include anxiety and irritation, then eventually vomiting, diarrhea, convulsions, or even a heart attack.

Heterosexual A person who chooses a member of the opposite sex as a romantic partner. See Human Sexuality.

Homosexual A person who chooses a member of the same sex as a romantic partner. See Human Sexuality.

Hormones Natural chemicals that cause various changes in your body. For example, a certain kind of hormone causes you to grow, another causes you to be afraid, and all kinds of hormones come into play when a woman has a baby. See Human Sexuality.

GLOSSARY

Hypertension High blood pressure—when the pressure of the blood on the walls of the vessels is too strong.

Indigestion A problem with digesting food. Symptoms usually include an uncomfortable feeling of fullness, heartburn, bloating, and nausea.

Inflammation The response of the body to irritation or injury: When the body is injured, it sends blood to the injured area to help mend it. For example, if you were to slam your hand in the car door, it would become inflammed. The symptoms of inflammation include redness, heat, swelling, and pain.

Inhale To breathe in.

Inherit To receive something from your ancestors. For example, your parents passed on certain biological traits to you through their genes: your hair color and type, your eye color, and your height. You can also inherit material goods—money, jewelry, books—from other people.

Insomnia Problems with getting to sleep—usually continuing over a long period of time.

Intoxication The state of being drunk caused by drinking too much alcohol.

Intravenous Referring to the inside of the blood vessels. For example, patients in the hospital often receive their food through an intravenous (IV) tube, inserted into a vein.

Inhibition The act of holding oneself in check. For example, if your parents are around, you might inhibited from kissing your boyfriend.

Juvenile delinquincy A violation of the law committed by a person who is not old enough to be considered an adult.

Kidneys The two organs that produce and eliminate urine. They are located in the back of the abdomen on either side of the spine.

Larynx Your voicebox, located between the throat and windpipe. You can feel your voicebox by touching your Adam's apple, the bump on the front of your neck.

Liquor A distilled alcoholic beverage, such as vodka. See also Distillation.

LSD Lysergic acid diethylamide. An illegal drug that affects the central nervous system.

Malnutrition A nutrition disorder. Malnutrition may be caused by the wrong kind of diet or the presence in the body of chemicals that prevent the absorption of certain nutrients.

Marijuana An illegal drug that comes from a hemp plant that is dried, then smoked. In a very few cases, marijuana is approved for use by cancer patients.

Mescaline A drug that comes from a part of the peyote, a Mexican cactus.

GLOSSARY

Metabolize To burn energy. Your body is always metabolizing. When you exercise, it metabolizes faster; when you sleep, it metabolizes slower.

Methadone A narcotic that is often used to alleviate the withdrawal symptoms of heroin addicts.

Morphine A narcotic that reduces pain. Morphine is legal when it is given by prescription.

Mucus The sticky, slippery material released by certain membranes and glands in the body. For example, mucus is found in the nose and the vagina. See Human Sexuality.

Narcotics A group of drugs made from opium poppies, an Eurasian plant. Repeated use of narcotics can be both physically and psychologically addictive.

Nausea A feeling that often leads to vomiting. For example, you might feel nauseous when you get car sick or when you eat too much.

Nicotine A colorless poison found in tobacco. Nicotine is one of the major reasons for the health problems caused by smoking.

Opium A drug that comes from the Eurasian opium poppy. See Narcotics.

Oxygen The name for the air you breathe. Technically, oxygen is a tasteless, odorless gas that humans can't live without.

Pancreas A gland located across the back of the abdomen, behind the stomach. The pancreas releases certain hormones and helps you to digest food.

Paranoia A feeling of suspiciousness, of not being able to trust anyone. For example, you're paranoid if you think everyone in your school is talking behind your back.

Passive smoking The act of breathing in the smoke from someone else's cigarette, pipe, or cigar.

PCP Phencyclidine hydrochloride—a drug that is often added to other drugs for a stronger effect. It may cause dizziness, nausea, flushing, sweating, and abnormal eye movement. An overdose could cause convulsions or death.

Peptic ulcer An ulcer of the stomach.

Peyote The Mexican cactus used to make mescaline.

Pneumonia An illness that involves swelling of the lungs, commonly caused by bacteria that has contaminated the lungs by breathing. Cigarette smoking can increase the risk of pneumonia by weakening the lungs so they can't fight off harmful bacteria.

Pot Slang name for marijuana. See Marijuana.

Prescription An order for drugs or treatment that is given by a doctor.

GLOSSARY

Proof The measure of the alcoholic content in an alcoholic drink.

Psilocybin A hallucinogenic drug that comes from a certain Mexican mushroom.

Psychiatric disorder A mental problem. Psychiatric disorders can be caused by genetics (family history), substance abuse, or environmental conditions.

Psychoactive drugs Drugs that affect the mind or behavior.

Respiratory system The system of organs that help you to breathe. The windpipe and lungs constitute the main parts of your respiratory system.

Seizure A convulsion or when a group of muscles react in a sudden, uncontrollable way. A seizure could be the result of a brain concussion.

Self-esteem Confidence in and satisfaction with yourself.

Solidified Something that has been made solid or hard. For example, ice is solidified water.

Stimulant A drug that increases the function levels of the body. For example, amphetamines make the heart beat faster.

Stroke A blood clot or bleeding in the brain that interferes with oxygen flow to the brain. Strokes can cause paralysis, speech defects, or even death.

Stupor A condition where a person lacks energy and does not care about his or her surroundings.

Substance abuse The overuse of and/or addiction to a chemical substance, such as tobacco, alcohol, or drugs. They lead to effects that are harmful to your health as well as the welfare of others.

Surgeon General The chief medical officer of a government health service. The United States has a Surgeon General who guides the country on decisions about what is healthy and what is not.

Syringe A device that injects or withdraws fluids. You know it as the "needle" that gives you a "shot."

Tar A brownish, sticky substance found in tobacco.

Taste buds The tiny organs distributed over the tongue and the roof of the mouth. Taste buds help you taste food.

Tetanus A potentially deadly infection of the nervous system. Because tetanus is caused by dangerous bacteria that enter an opening in the skin, your doctor will often recommend a tetanus shot after you cut yourself.

Tobacco A plant whose leaves are dried and then smoked or chewed.

Tranquilizers Drugs that reduce anxiety.

GLOSSARY

Ulcer A break in the skin or in a mucous membrane—like a sore. When most people think of ulcers, they think of peptic ulcers, which occur in the stomach.

Vapor A gaseous substance

Viral infections Diseases that are caused by viruses. A virus is a tiny organism that enters the body through cuts in the skin, through breathing, or through eating. Some viral infections are dangerous; others aren't.

Windpipe See Breathing Tract.

USEFUL ADDRESSES AND ORGANIZATIONS

Addiction Research and Treatment Corporation
22 Chapel St.
Brooklyn, NY 11201

Al-Anon Family Group Headquarters
P.O. Box 182
New York, NY 10159

Alcohol, Drug Abuse, and Mental Health Administration
5600 Fishers Ln.
Rockville, MD 20857

Alcohol and Drug Problems Association of North America
444 North Capitol N.W.
Suite 181
Washington, D.C. 20001

Alcohol Education for Youth and Community
362 State St.
Albany, NY 12210

Alcoholics Anonymous
P.O. Box 459
Grand Central Station
New York, NY 10163

American Cancer Society
19 West 56th St.
New York, NY 10019

American Council on Alcoholism
8501 LaSalle Rd.
Suite 301
Towson, MD 21204

American Council for Drug Education
5820 Hubbard Dr.
Rockville, MD 20852

American Health Association
320 East 43rd St.
New York, NY 10017

American Heart Association
7320 Greenville Ave.
Dallas, TX 75231

Americans United for a Smoke Free Society
3050 K Street N.W.
Washington, D.C. 20007

Breathe Free Plan to Stop Smoking
6830 Laurel St. N.W.
Washington, D.C. 20012

Children of Alcoholics Foundation
200 Park Ave.
New York, NY 10166

Coalition on Smoking or Health
1607 New Hampshire Ave. N.W.
Washington, D.C. 20009

Committees of Correspondence
57 Conant St.
Room 113
Danvers, MA 01923

Do It Now Foundation
P.O. Box 21126
Phoenix, AZ 85036

Drug-Anon Focus
P.O. Box 9108
Long Island City, NY 11103

Drugs Anonymous
P.O. Box 473
Ansonia Station
New York, NY 10023

Ethos Foundation
Three Skyline Pl.
5201 Leesburg Pike, Suite 100
Falls Church, VA 22041

Families in Action National Drug Information Center
3845 North Druid Hills Rd.
Suite 300
Decatur, GA 30033

Families Anonymous
P.O. Box 528
Van Nuys, CA 91408

Group Against Smokers Pollution (GASP)
P.O. Box 632
College Park, MD 20740

Just Say No Clubs
c/o Oakland Parents in Action
1404 Franklin St., Suite 610
Oakland, CA 94612

Narcotic Educational Foundation of America
5055 Sunset Blvd.
Los Angeles, CA 90027

Narcotics Anonymous
P.O. Box 9999
Van Nuys, CA 91406

Narcotics Education, Inc.
6830 Laurel St. N.W.
Washington, D.C. 20012

National Association on Drug Abuse Problems
355 Lexington Ave.
New York, NY 10017

National Association of State Alcohol and Drug Abuse
444 North Capitol St. N.W.
Suite 530
Washington, D.C. 20001

National Clearinghouse for Alcohol Information
P.O. Box 2345
Rockville, MD 20852

National Clearinghouse for Drug Abuse Information
P.O. Box 416
Department DQ
Kensington, MD 20795

National Clearinghouse for Smoking and Health
Westwood Towers, Room 500
5401 Westbard Ave.
Bethesda, MD 20016

National Council on Alcoholism
12 West 21st St.
New York, NY 10010

National Institute on Drug Abuse
11400 Rockville Pike
Room 110
Rockville, MD 20852

National Prevention Network
444 North Capitol St. N.W.
Suite 530
Washington, D.C. 20001

Office on Smoking and Health
Technical Information Center
Park Building, Room 116
5600 Fishers Ln.
Rockville, MD 20857

Potsmokers Anonymous
316 East Third St.
New York, NY 10009

Reach Out
14950 444th Ave. S.E.
North Bend, WA 98045

Smokenders
18551 Von Karmen Ave.
Irvine, CA 92715

Target: Helping Students Cope with Alcohol and Drugs
P.O. Box 20626
11724 Plaza Cir.
Kansas City, MO 64195

War on Drugs
5456 Lake Ave.
Sanford, FL 32771

INDEX